NOTICE: You !
Reprint c

COPYRIGHT© 2010-2023 JKW Enterprises, Inc. All Rights Reserved:

Disclaimer and/or Legal Notices:

This book is intended to provide general information about the subject matter covered. It is sold with the understanding that the author and publisher are not engaged in rendering professional services. If professional advice or other expert assistance is required, the services of a competent professional should be sought. The author and publisher have made every effort to ensure the accuracy of the information herein. However, the information contained in this book is provided 'as is' without warranty of any kind. The publisher is not responsible for any errors or omissions, or for the results obtained from the use of this information. All information in this book is provided with no guarantee of completeness, accuracy, timeliness or of the results obtained from the use of this information, and without warranty of any kind, express or implied. The recipes contained in this book are to be followed exactly as written. The publisher is not responsible for any specific health or allergy needs that may require medical supervision and are not liable for any damages or negative consequences from any treatment, action, application, or preparation, to any person reading or following the information in this book. It is always recommended to consult with a healthcare professional before starting any diet, exercise, or supplementation program, before taking any medication, or if you have or suspect you might have a health problem. No part of this book may be reproduced or transmitted in any form or by any means, electronic or mechanical, including photocopying, recording, or by any information storage and retrieval system, without written permission from the author, except for the inclusion of brief quotations in a review.

Introduction: Homesteading—The Path to True Self-Reliance..............3

Chapter 1: Planning Your Homestead 5

Chapter 2: Finding the Right Spot—More Than Just a Pretty View........8

Chapter 3: Landscaping and Building Infrastructure 13

Chapter 4: Creating a Fully Functional Garden 16

Chapter 5: Composting and Recycling. 22

Chapter 6: The Bounty of Your Garden 25

Chapter 7: Livestock, Poultry and Other Critters 32

Chapter 8: Harvesting & Preserving 38

Chapter 9: Daily Production & Beekeeping 43

Chapter 10: Off the Grid Power, Water & Sanitation..........................47

Chapter 11: Essential Homesteading Skills..53

Chapter 12: Taking the Leap to Self-Reliance.....................................59

INTRODUCTION: HOMESTEADING—THE PATH TO TRUE SELF-RELIANCE

Well now, pull up a chair and lend an ear, my friend. We've got a journey ahead, one that will take us back to the wisdom of our ancestors, but with a fine-tuned focus on our future. Y'see, there's an old saying my grandpappy used to repeat, "Folks are usually about as happy as they make up their minds to be." Abraham Lincoln, I believe, first said that. And I reckon it's high time we decided to be self-reliant, and not just happy, but downright jubilant in the process.

In this fast-paced world we live in, it's become second nature to depend on others. We rely on trucks to bring our food, power companies for our electricity, and often, we look to the government for assistance when times get tough. But what happens if that truck doesn't show up one day? Or if the lights flicker and go out, and stay out? It's not about fear, mind you. It's about being ready, come what may. As the old Boy Scout motto goes, "Be Prepared."

Self-reliance, my dear reader, isn't just a lofty ideal—it's a necessity. By cultivating our own food, creating our own power, and learning the time-honored skills of our ancestors, we place our destiny back into our own hands. Now, I'm not saying it's easy; truth be told, it's quite the opposite. But as my old Ma used to say, "Ain't no hill too steep for a stepper." And that's what we aim to be—steppers, doers, builders of our own destiny.

Just take a gander at the world around us, and you'll see why this journey towards self-reliance is so crucial. From global pandemics to climate changes, from political unrest to economic instability—it's clear that there are mighty rough waters ahead. No one wants to be the chicken caught in the rain, so to speak, and that's where the principles of homesteading come in.

This ain't about running away from modern life. On the contrary, it's about integrating the wisdom of our ancestors with the conveniences of today to build a self-sustaining and enriching lifestyle. It's about being ready for those hard times and knowing that, no matter what happens around you, you've got the knowledge and skills to weather the storm.

I hope you're itching to roll up your sleeves and get your hands dirty because what we're embarking on is a return to fundamentals, a journey of resilience, resourcefulness, and independence. Homesteading ain't just about land or livestock—it's a state of mind. It's the spirit of standing on your own two feet and the satisfaction of providing for yourself and your loved ones.

So join me, won't you, on this path less traveled, as we dig into the secrets of our ancestors and unlock the wisdom of the land. Let's take the reins and become masters of our own destiny. As we turn the pages of this book, remember: every journey begins with a single step, and this here's ours.

Well then, let's get started, shall we? No time like the present, as they say.

Stay tuned, partner, the road to self-reliance is about to get interesting. Let's hitch up our wagons and blaze a trail together towards a life less dependent and more fulfilled. The old ways are whispering in the wind, it's high time we start listening.

CHAPTER 1: PLANNING YOUR HOMESTEAD

Well now, aren't we getting right down to brass tacks? I'm mightily pleased to see that enthusiasm, partner! Before we hitch up our britches and dive in, let's talk planning. You see, as the old saying goes, "Measure twice, cut once." A little time spent with pencil and paper now could save a heap of heartache down the road.

Planning your homestead is like drawing a map for a journey. It gives you a clear route to follow and helps you foresee potential obstacles. It also helps set achievable goals and allows you to pace yourself. Your homestead is a living, breathing entity, and like any creature, it will grow and change with time. This plan, it's more of a guideline than a set-in-stone rule book.

Now, the first step in planning is to envision your homestead. Close your eyes for a spell and imagine what you want your homestead to look like. Do you see lush green fields with chickens pecking at the ground, a red barn housing a couple of Jersey cows, a vegetable patch with tomatoes ripe for picking, or maybe a couple of beehives buzzing with activity?

What about water? A homesteader without water is like a hen without feathers—mighty exposed and in a heap of trouble. Do you have a natural water source on your property, or will you need to dig a well? How about rainwater collection?

Consider your energy sources. Will you harness the power of the sun with solar panels, or the strength of the wind with turbines? Maybe there's a swift-moving stream on your land you can use for hydroelectric power. And let's not forget about good old-fashioned wood for heating and cooking.

Livestock, too, should be a part of your vision. Chickens, goats, cows, pigs, or maybe even bees for honey—it all depends on your homesteading goals. Just remember, as my ma used to say, "Don't buy a pig in a poke." In other words, know what you're getting into before you commit.

The goal here ain't to build Rome in a day. Think of it as laying the first stone. Rome wasn't built overnight, and your homestead won't be either. Your initial goals should be realistic and achievable. Start with the essentials—shelter, water, food production, and waste management (that's where composting comes in).

Once those bases are covered, think about transportation. Will you have a horse for riding, a bicycle for short trips, or will you need a vehicle? Remember, every horse has to be fed, and every engine needs fuel.

The goal of homesteading is self-sufficiency, and that includes financial independence. What skills do you have that could generate an income? Do you make a killer apple butter that locals would line up for? Maybe you're handy with a sewing needle or a whiz at repairing machinery. Put those talents to work for you on your homestead.

By taking the time to envision and plan your homestead, you're doing more than just dreaming—you're building a future. Make your plan flexible enough to adapt to challenges and changes. Because, as any old-timer can tell you, "The best-laid plans of mice and men often go awry."

But don't let that discourage you. We're made of stern stuff, us homesteaders. We know how to roll with the punches and keep our chins up. Remember, a smooth sea never made a skilled sailor, and a few bumps in the road can only make us stronger.

So, my friend, grab that pencil, pull out that paper, and let's get to planning your homestead. It's the first step on this incredible journey to self-reliance. The road might be long and winding, but I promise you, the view from the end is worth every step.

Here's a simple table to help you plan your homestead. You can use it as a guide to structure your homesteading goals and to keep track of your progress.

Category	Goals	Action Steps	Timeline
Shelter	Example: Build a cabin	List out each step required to accomplish the goal, e.g., 1. Design cabin layout, 2. Collect construction materials, etc.	Set achievable deadlines for each step, e.g., Design by July, Construction begins in August, etc.
Water	Example: Install a rainwater collection system	List out each step required to accomplish the goal	Set achievable deadlines for each step
Food Production	Example: Plant a vegetable garden	List out each step required to accomplish the goal	Set achievable deadlines for each step
Waste Management	Example: Set up composting system	List out each step required to accomplish the goal	Set achievable deadlines for each step

Category	Goals	Action Steps	Timeline
Energy	Example: Install solar panels	List out each step required to accomplish the goal	Set achievable deadlines for each step
Livestock	Example: Raise chickens for eggs	List out each step required to accomplish the goal	Set achievable deadlines for each step
Transportation	Example: Maintain bicycle for local travel	List out each step required to accomplish the goal	Set achievable deadlines for each step
Income Generation	Example: Sell homemade apple butter	List out each step required to accomplish the goal	Set achievable deadlines for each step

Now, to use this table effectively, start by jotting down your homesteading goals for each category. Be realistic and consider your resources, both in terms of time and finances.

Next, break down each goal into smaller, actionable steps. This will make your goals seem less daunting and more manageable.

Finally, set a timeline for each action step. This helps keep you on track and allows you to monitor your progress. But remember, these timelines are just guides. Don't beat yourself up if things don't go exactly as planned. As we've said, homesteading is a journey, not a race.

Keep this table handy and refer to it regularly. Update it as you accomplish your goals and as new goals emerge. It's a living document, just like your homestead.

Homesteading Secrets of Our Ancestors | Page 7

CHAPTER 2: FINDING THE RIGHT SPOT—MORE THAN JUST A PRETTY VIEW

Well, now that we've got our plan all laid out, let's talk about the next step—finding the right spot for your homestead. "Location, location, location" ain't just a catchphrase for real estate agents. When it comes to homesteading, it can make or break your success. So, sit back, pull your hat down low, and let's dig into this crucial decision.

SECTION 1: WHAT TO LOOK FOR IN A HOMESTEAD

Choosing the right piece of land for your homestead is like picking a good apple. Now, let's ponder that apple a bit more.

You see, the shiniest apple ain't always the best one. It could be all show and no substance. A few spots and blemishes, on the other hand, can be overlooked if the flavor and texture are just right. It's about knowing what matters most. Your homestead is much the same.

You'll likely need to compromise on a few things, but knowing what's non-negotiable is the key to making a wise choice. Now, here are some aspects you might need to ponder on:

Access to Water: This here is a must. A homestead without water is like a fish without fins—it just won't work. You'll need water for your home, garden, livestock, and maybe even for some small-scale hydroelectric power. If there ain't a reliable, clean source of water on the property, it could be a deal-breaker. However, if there's a chance to dig a well or set up rainwater harvesting, it could be a compromise worth considering.

The Lay of the Land: Ideal homestead land is relatively flat for building and planting. But remember, even the Rock of Gibraltar wasn't built in a day. You can slowly but surely level out a hilly patch for cultivation or build a house on stilts if the land is a bit uneven. But if the land is too steep or marshy, you may be buying a peck of trouble.

Sun Exposure: Plenty of sunlight is essential for crops and can also power your homestead if you're considering solar energy. A property with dense forest might look idyllic, but if the sun can't find its way to your vegetable patch, you're in a pickle. You can compromise by clearing a few trees, but if the property is in the shadow of a hill or building, it may be best to tip your hat and move on.

Soil Quality: While you can improve soil fertility over time with compost and crop rotation, starting with barren or polluted soil is like trying to make a silk purse out of a sow's ear—it's an uphill battle. Soil testing is essential before purchasing land. If the soil's poor but the other aspects are tickety-boo, you could compromise by planning to invest time and resources in building up the soil.

Potential Hazards: This is another non-negotiable. Avoid areas prone to natural disasters like floods or wildfires. Sure, as my pappy used to say, "You can't keep trouble from visiting, but you don't have to offer it a chair." If the risk is minimal or can be mitigated, it might be a compromise you're willing to make.

Remember, just like picking that apple, choosing your homestead will require a little give-and-take. And as you weigh these factors, keep in mind the old adage, "You can't make a racehorse out of a pig. But if you work hard enough, you can make a mighty fast pig." In other words, with a bit of patience, effort, and compromise, you can turn a less-than-perfect piece of land into a homestead that's just right for you.

SECTION 2: TIPS FOR BUYING LAND

As we've established, buying land for your homestead is not a decision to be rushed. Just like you wouldn't buy a horse without checking its teeth, don't purchase land without a thorough inspection and investigation. Here's some wisdom on the nitty-gritty of the buying process.

Finding Good Land: In today's world, there are plenty of tools at your disposal to help find that perfect patch of soil. You can start with online real estate platforms that let you filter properties based on your preferences. Engage with local communities, farmers, or homesteading groups—they often have the best leads and invaluable local knowledge. Visit local markets, fairs, or county extension offices. As the saying goes, "Shake the hand that feeds you." Building local relationships can yield rich dividends.

Check the Property's Title and Boundaries: Make sure the property's title is clear—that means it's free of any disputes or claims. Hire a professional to conduct a land survey. This will give you an accurate understanding of the property's boundaries, and it could reveal any potential issues like encroachments by neighbors.

Ensure There Are No Liens: A lien is a claim made by a third party on a property due to the owner's unpaid debt. If a property has a lien, it could become your problem after purchase. Your attorney can help you ensure that the property is free of any liens.

Understand Loan Terms: If you're financing your purchase, make sure you understand the terms of the loan. What's the interest rate? How long is the term? Are there any penalties for early payment? As we often say, "Read the fine print; it's where the devil hides."

Negotiating the Purchase: Negotiation is a bit like a barn dance—it takes two to tango. Don't be afraid to negotiate the price based on your research and the property's pros and cons. If you're not comfortable doing this yourself, consider hiring a professional or a savvy friend to help. Remember, "You catch more flies with honey than vinegar." Be respectful, but firm.

Buying Without a Realtor: Buying land without a realtor can save you a pretty penny, but it's not without its challenges. You'll need to handle all the tasks a realtor would usually do. This includes finding properties, negotiating prices, handling paperwork, and understanding legal requirements. If you choose this path, it's highly recommended to hire a good real estate attorney to guide you. You might also consider a real estate course or extensive reading to understand the process better.

Above all, keep this old adage in mind: "Measure twice, cut once." In other words, be thorough in your investigations and assessments. A bit of patience and prudence now could save you a world of trouble down the road.

SECTION 3: LOCAL LAWS AND ZONING

Just like you can't plant taters in the winter and expect a crop come spring, you can't just plunk your homestead down anywhere without considering local laws and zoning regulations. These dictate what you can and can't do on your property. Here's what to look for:

Residential Zoning: Is the land zoned for residential use? You'll need this if you plan on building a home or even just a tiny house on wheels. If the land is zoned for agriculture or commercial use, you may have to jump through a few hoops to get a permit for a dwelling.

Agricultural Activities: This includes farming, gardening, and keeping livestock. Some zones are persnickety about what animals you can keep and how many. Be sure to check if you can have chickens, cows, pigs, bees, etc. In some places, even a veggie garden might be a no-no if it's in the front yard.

Additional Structures: Planning on building a barn, a shed, a greenhouse, a workshop, or a root cellar? Some zones limit the number and type of structures you can build, or even their size and placement.

Home Business: If you plan to sell your farm produce, offer farm stays, run workshops, or have any other form of on-site business, you need to check the local regulations. Some zones prohibit home businesses or place restrictions on them.

Water and Waste Management: Do you have the rights to use the water on your land? This might affect your ability to irrigate your garden, water your livestock, or even your home use. And then there's waste management—are you allowed to compost? Can you install a septic system or an outhouse?

Renewable Energy Systems: If you're planning to generate your own electricity using solar panels, wind turbines, or a micro-hydro system, check if local laws support or restrict these.

To find all this out, a good place to start is your local county or municipal office. They can provide zoning maps and ordinances. Also, don't forget the power of community—talk to neighbors, join local groups, or attend local meetings. These folks have been around the block and can offer a wealth of knowledge.

If the zoning laws in your chosen area are too restrictive for your homesteading plans, it's like trying to squeeze a square peg into a round hole. No matter how much you love the land, you may need to move on and find a place where your dreams can take root and grow. As the old saying goes, "There's no use flogging a dead horse."

SECTION 4: CHECKING LAND FERTILITY—DON'T TRY TO PLOW A FIELD BY TURNING IT OVER IN YOUR MIND

Your homestead's soil is like the kitchen of your farm—it's where all the magic happens. A rich, healthy soil will provide the most succulent vegetables, the tallest corn, and the juiciest fruits. Here's how to get a gauge on your soil's fertility:

Conduct a Soil Test: You can buy a simple soil test kit from most garden centers or online. This will tell you about the soil's pH and nutrient levels. You're looking for a near-neutral pH (6 to 7) and a good balance of nutrients like nitrogen, phosphorus, and potassium.

Observe the Land: Is it covered in lush, healthy vegetation? Are there worms and other critters when you dig a bit? These are good signs. If the land is barren, or plants and trees look stunted and unhealthy, you might have a bit of work on your hands.

Feel the Soil: Is it loose and crumbly, or hard and compacted? Does it hold together when you squeeze a handful, then crumble again when you touch it? That's ideal.

Remember what my pappy used to say: "Soil is the stomach of the plant." You can always improve soil over time by adding compost, manure, or other amendments, but starting with good soil will save you a heap of work and heartache. Treat your soil with respect—it's the breadbasket of your homestead.

SECTION 5: UNDERSTANDING LOCAL WEATHER AND CLIMATE—THERE'S NO SUCH THING AS BAD WEATHER, ONLY DIFFERENT KINDS OF GOOD WEATHER

Mother Nature is a fickle mistress—she giveth, and she taketh away. Knowing your local weather and climate is like understanding her moods. It'll guide you in picking the right crops, planning your water needs, building your structures, and preparing for her tantrums.

- **Average Rainfall and Temperature:** These will influence what crops you can grow, when you can plant and harvest, and how much watering your garden will need.
- **Common Natural Disasters:** Are wildfires, floods, hurricanes, tornadoes, heavy snowfall, or drought common in the area? You'll need to plan and prepare for these.
- **Length of Growing Season:** This determines what crops you can grow. Some plants need a long, warm growing season, while others prefer a short, cool one.
- **Sun Exposure:** Does the property get plenty of sunshine, or is it mostly in the shade? You'll need at least six hours of direct sunlight for most crops.
- **Wind:** Constant, strong winds can damage crops, erode soil, and make it hard to maintain a comfortable temperature in your home. A sheltered spot is ideal.

Just remember, every cloud has a silver lining, and even the toughest weather can be harnessed for your benefit with a bit of planning and ingenuity. As old Jed used to say, "You can't change the wind, but you can adjust your sails."

Remember, finding the right spot for your homestead is as much a matter of heart as it is of head. Listen to your instincts, but let your common sense have the final say. And always remember the words of that old cowboy: "Don't squat with your spurs on." In other words, don't make life harder than it needs to be. Choose wisely, and you'll be well on your way to creating the homestead of your dreams.

CHAPTER 3: LANDSCAPING AND BUILDING INFRASTRUCTURE

Welcome to the next leg of your homesteading journey—landscaping and building your farmstead. It's like what my mama used to say about making a quilt: "It's a piece of your heart stitched with love." Let's break it down into pieces you can stitch together.

SECTION 1: LANDSCAPING—DON'T DIG A PIT FOR OTHERS; YOU MIGHT FALL INTO IT YOURSELF

Landscaping ain't just about making your homestead look pretty—it's about making it work for you. The lay of your land can help or hinder your homesteading efforts, so plan wisely.

- **Terrain:** Flat, slightly sloped, or hilly? Each has its advantages and disadvantages. Flat areas are great for building and gardening, slopes can be perfect for orchards or vineyards, and hills can offer wind protection and good drainage.
- **Drainage:** You want your land to drain well to prevent water-logging in your garden or around your buildings. At the same time, you want to conserve as much water as you can. Swales, trenches, and rain gardens can help with both.
- **Microclimates:** Use these to your advantage. A south-facing slope will be warmer and sunnier than a north-facing one. A dip in the terrain can form a frost pocket. A wall or fence can create a heat trap.
- **Windbreaks and Shade:** Plant trees or build structures to provide protection from wind, and offer shade where needed.

Remember, good landscaping is like training a vine—it guides your homestead to grow in the right direction.

SECTION 2: BUILDING YOUR DWELLING—YOU CAN'T BUILD A HOUSE WITH A SINGLE NAIL

Whether it's a farmhouse, a tiny house, or a cabin, your dwelling is the heart of your homestead. It's where you'll retreat after a day's work, cook your meals, and rest your weary bones. Here are some things to consider:

- **Size and Design:** Think about your needs, your lifestyle, and your future plans. It's easier to build a little extra space now than to add it on later. Consider a design that allows for passive solar heating and cooling to save on energy costs.
- **Materials:** Local, natural materials like stone, clay, straw, and wood can be cheaper, more sustainable, and more in harmony with your surroundings.

- **Placement:** Your house should be easily accessible, but also in a safe, secure location. Consider sun exposure, wind direction, noise, privacy, and proximity to your barn, garden, and other structures.

SECTION 3: BUILDING YOUR BARN, SHEDS, AND PENS—A GOOD FARMER MAKES A GOOD BARN

A barn for your livestock, sheds for your tools, and pens for your chickens or pigs are important structures on your homestead. Just like you can't put the cart before the horse, you've got to build these right:

- **Location:** Place your barn and pens so they're easy to access in all weather, but far enough to keep noises, smells, and flies away from your house.
- **Size and Design:** Make sure they're big enough for your needs, but not so big that you're wasting materials and space. Think about ventilation, light, temperature control, and ease of cleaning and maintenance.
- **Fencing:** Good fences make good neighbors, and good pens. They keep your animals in and predators out. Consider the needs of your animals and the local wildlife when choosing your fencing.

Remember, every nail holds a story. The more thought and care you put into your structures, the more they'll give back to you.

SECTION 4: PROTECTIVE STRUCTURES—PREPARE AND PREVENT, DON'T REPAIR AND REPENT

Your homestead is your castle, and every castle needs its defenses.

- **Fencing:** Not just for your animals, but also for your garden to keep out critters, and for your property to mark boundaries.
- **Greenhouses and Cold Frames:** These can extend your growing season, protect your crops from harsh weather, and give you a place to start seedlings.
- **Storm Shelters and Cellars:** Depending on your local weather, you might need a safe place to hide during a storm, or a cool, dark place to store your harvest.

Building your homestead is like a journey of a thousand miles—it begins with a single step. Each day, you put one foot in front of the other, and before you know it, you've reached your destination. Happy building, friend.

SECTION 5: CULTIVATING YOUR LAND

Cultivating your land ain't just about turning the soil and sowing the seeds—it's about creating a living, breathing ecosystem that sustains you, your animals, and the natural flora and fauna. Here's how to get started:

- **Preparing the Soil:** Just as a potter prepares his clay, you need to prepare your soil. Start by clearing any debris like rocks, roots, and weeds. Then, till or turn the soil to break it up and improve aeration and drainage. If the soil is poor, you might need to add compost or other organic matter to enrich it.
- **Planning Your Garden:** Think about what you want to grow, how much space each plant needs, and when to plant and harvest. Consider companion planting, which is like setting up a friendly neighborhood for your plants—they help each other grow better. Don't forget about crop rotation to keep your soil healthy and prevent diseases.
- **Planting:** Whether you're sowing seeds or planting seedlings, make sure to give each plant enough space to grow. Plant in rows or beds for easier care and harvesting. Remember, slow and steady wins the race—don't rush, and plant with care.
- **Watering and Mulching:** Regular watering is essential, especially in the early stages of growth. But remember, too much of a good thing can be bad—don't drown your plants. Mulch helps to conserve moisture, control weeds, and add organic matter to the soil.
- **Weeding and Pest Control:** Weeds are like uninvited guests—they eat your food and make a mess. Regular weeding keeps them in check. Use natural methods like traps, barriers, and beneficial insects for pest control. As granny used to say, "Prevention is better than cure."

Cultivating your land is like tending a newborn—it needs your time, patience, and love. But the fruits of your labor will be as sweet as the juiciest peach, and as satisfying as a hard day's work.

CHAPTER 4: CREATING A FULLY FUNCTIONAL GARDEN

As I always say, a good homesteader's wealth is in his garden. So, let's learn how to cultivate that wealth.

SECTION 1: GARDEN LAYOUT AND DESIGN—PLAN BEFORE YOU PLANT

Just like you wouldn't build a house without a blueprint, don't start a garden without a plan.

- **Size and Location:** Consider how much time you can devote and how much food you want to produce. You want a sunny spot, close to your house for easy care and harvesting.
- **Beds or Rows:** Beds are easier to maintain, but rows can make better use of space for some crops.
- **Paths:** Make sure you have easy access to all your plants without stepping on the soil.
- **Rotation and Succession:** Plan to rotate crops each year to prevent diseases and improve soil fertility. Succession planting can give you a continuous harvest.

Here's an example of a garden plan for a quarter-acre homestead:

Plant	Seed Quantity	Row Distance	Amount/ Person	Plant Spacing
Beans	200-250 seeds	18-24 inches	10-15 plants	4-6 inches
Beets	1000-1500 seeds	12-18 inches	15-20 plants	3-4 inches
Carrots	1000-2000 seeds	12-18 inches	10-15 plants	2-3 inches
Corn	100-150 seeds	30-36 inches	12-15 plants	9-12 inches
Cucumbers	50-75 seeds	36-60 inches	2-3 plants	1-2 feet
Lettuce	400-600 seeds	12-18 inches	5-7 plants	8-12 inches
Onions	300-500 sets	12-18 inches	10-15 plants	4-6 inches
Peppers	50-75 seeds	18-24 inches	2-3 plants	1-2 feet
Potatoes	15-20 tubers	30-36 inches	5-10 plants	12-15 inches
Squash	25-35 seeds	48-60 inches	1-2 plants	2-3 feet

Plant	Seed Quantity	Row Distance	Amount/ Person	Plant Spacing
Tomatoes	25-35 seeds	36-48 inches	2-3 plants	2-3 feet
Broccoli	50-75 seeds	18-24 inches	3-5 plants	18-20 inches
Cabbage	50-75 seeds	24-30 inches	3-5 plants	18-24 inches
Cauliflower	50-75 seeds	24-30 inches	3-5 plants	18-24 inches
Swiss Chard	100-150 seeds	18-24 inches	5-7 plants	6-8 inches
Radishes	800-1000 seeds	12-18 inches	20-30 plants	1-2 inches
Peas	200-250 seeds	18-24 inches	20-30 plants	1-2 inches
Spinach	200-300 seeds	12-18 inches	10-20 plants	3-4 inches
Zucchini	25-35 seeds	48-60 inches	1-2 plants	2-3 feet
Eggplant	25-35 seeds	18-24 inches	1-2 plants	2-3 feet
Kale	100-150 seeds	18-24 inches	5-7 plants	8-12 inches
Pumpkin	25-35 seeds	60-96 inches	1-2 plants	4-6 feet
Watermelon	25-35 seeds	60-96 inches	1-2 plants	4-6 feet
Sweet Potato	50-60 slips	36-48 inches	5-10 plants	12-15 inches
Turnip	200-300 seeds	12-18 inches	5-10 plants	2-3 inches
Okra	50-75 seeds	24-36 inches	5-10 plants	12-18 inches

Please remember that these are just ballpark numbers. Some plants might require more space or different conditions depending on specific varieties and the region where you're planting. Gardening is a learning process, don't be discouraged if everything isn't perfect right off the bat. As they say, "The best fertilizer is the gardener's shadow." That means the more attention and care you give your garden, the more it will grow.

SECTION 2: SOIL PREPARATION—GOOD SOIL, GOOD HARVEST

A gardener's best friend is his compost pile. Here's a checklist for how to get your soil ready:

- ✓ **Identify your soil type**: Is it sandy, clay, silt, or a mix? Understanding your soil type will help you know what amendments you might need.
- ✓ **Test your soil**: This can tell you about its pH and nutrient levels. You can get a soil testing kit at most garden stores or send a sample to a local extension service.
- ✓ **Remove weeds and debris**: Get rid of any rocks, sticks, and other debris. Pull up any existing weeds by the root.
- ✓ **Add organic matter**: Organic matter, like compost or well-rotted manure, can improve soil structure, moisture retention, and nutrient availability.
- ✓ **Till or turn the soil**: Break up compacted soil with a tiller or garden fork. This will make it easier for plant roots to grow.
- ✓ **Apply soil amendments**: Based on your soil test results, you might need to add specific nutrients or adjust the pH with lime or sulfur.
- ✓ **Create garden beds**: Raised beds, rows, or mounds can improve drainage and increase soil temperature.
- ✓ **Install irrigation**: Depending on your garden size and location, this might be as simple as a watering can, or you might want to install drip irrigation.
- ✓ **Set up a compost area**: This can be a simple pile or a constructed compost bin. It's a great way to recycle kitchen scraps and yard waste into rich compost.
- ✓ **Plan your plantings**: Consider things like sunlight, plant height, and companion planting when deciding where each plant will go.
- ✓ **Purchase seeds or seedlings**: Make sure you're ready to plant when the time and conditions are right.
- ✓ **Install supports**: For climbing plants like beans and tomatoes, set up trellises or stakes before or at planting time.
- ✓ **Prepare for pests**: Have a plan for dealing with common garden pests. This might include fencing, netting, or organic pesticides.
- ✓ **Gather tools**: Make sure you have all the necessary tools clean and in good repair. This might include a spade, hoe, rake, trowel, pruning shears, and a wheelbarrow.

Remember, "The garden was not made in a day." Patience and care are your best tools in the garden. Take the time to prepare properly, and you'll be rewarded with a bounty of fresh food.

SECTION 3: PLANTING AND MAINTENANCE—IT'S A LABOR OF LOVE

Planting your garden is like starting a new chapter in a book. You're filled with hope and excitement for what's to come.

- **Choosing Plants:** Choose a mix of fruits, vegetables, herbs, and flowers. Look for varieties adapted to your climate and resistant to local pests and diseases.
- **Sowing Seeds or Planting Seedlings:** Follow the instructions for each plant regarding depth, spacing, and timing.
- **Watering, Weeding, and Mulching**: Regular watering, weeding, and mulching will keep your plants happy and healthy.

SECTION 4: COMPANION GARDENING—PLANTS LIKE GOOD NEIGHBORS, TOO

Some plants grow better together, while others don't get along. Companion planting can improve plant health and yield, and help with pest control.

Learn which plants are friends and which are foes. For instance, tomatoes love basil but hate potatoes.

Below is a chart of the top 25 plants for your homestead garden and the good and bad plants to grow along side them.

Plant	Good Companions	Bad Companions
Tomatoes	Basil, Marigold, Carrots, Asparagus, Parsley	Potatoes, Corn, Kohlrabi
Cucumbers	Corn, Sunflowers, Radishes, Peas, Beans	Aromatic herbs (like sage), Potatoes
Beans	Corn, Cucumbers, Marigolds, Sunflowers	Onions, Garlic, Shallots, Leeks
Carrots	Tomatoes, Peas, Lettuce, Onions, Sage	Dill, Celery
Peas	Corn, Beans, Carrots, Radishes, Turnips	Onions, Garlic, Shallots, Leeks
Lettuce	Carrots, Radishes, Cucumbers, Strawberries	Broccoli, Brussels sprouts, Cabbage
Corn	Beans, Cucumbers, Squash	Tomatoes
Broccoli	Onions, Beets, Marigolds, Nasturtium	Strawberries, Tomatoes, Mustard
Squash	Corn, Beans, Radishes	Potatoes
Radishes	Peas, Lettuce, Cucumbers	Hyssop
Onions	Beets, Carrots, Lettuce, Cabbage	Beans, Peas
Beets	Onions, Kohlrabi, Cabbage	Pole beans, Mustard
Spinach	Radishes, Strawberries, Cabbage	Potatoes

Plant	Good Companions	Bad Companions
Cabbage	Beets, Celery, Onions, Potatoes	Strawberries, Tomatoes, Dill
Potatoes	Beans, Cabbage, Horseradish, Marigolds	Carrots, Tomatoes, Cucumbers, Sunflowers
Cauliflower	Beans, Celery, Oregano	Strawberries, Tomatoes
Asparagus	Basil, Parsley, Tomatoes	Garlic, Potatoes, Onions
Eggplant	Beans, Peppers, Potatoes	Fennel
Peppers	Basil, Onions, Spinach, Tomatoes	Fennel, Kohlrabi
Zucchini	Corn, Marigold, Radishes	Potatoes
Pumpkin	Corn, Beans	Potatoes
Celery	Cabbage, Tomatoes, Leeks	Carrots, Parsley
Parsley	Tomatoes, Asparagus, Corn	Lettuce
Sunflowers	Cucumbers, Corn, Beans	Potatoes
Strawberries	Bush Beans, Spinach, Borage	Cabbage, Broccoli, Cauliflower

SECTION 5: PEST CONTROL—AN OUNCE OF PREVENTION IS WORTH A POUND OF CURE

A healthy garden can fend off most pests, but sometimes you need to lend a hand.

Natural Predators: Attracting natural predators is like hiring a private security force for your garden. Birds, frogs, and beneficial insects all feed on common pests. Planting a variety of flowers and providing habitats like birdhouses, small ponds, and insect hotels can attract these helpful creatures. And let's not forget about our friend the garden spider. They might look scary, but they're the best pest control you can ask for. Remember, "The enemy of my enemy is my friend."

Barriers and Traps: Sometimes, the best offense is a good defense. Consider physical barriers like netting for fruit trees, collars for young plants, and row covers for vulnerable crops. Slug and snail traps, often filled with beer, can protect tender greens. If larger critters are a problem, consider a good strong fence. An old farming adage goes, "Good fences make good neighbors."

Organic Sprays: If the bugs are really bugging you, there are a variety of organic sprays you can try. Diatomaceous earth, neem oil, and insecticidal soaps can be quite effective. Homemade sprays using garlic, chili powder, or vinegar can also deter pests. Just remember, "You catch more flies with honey than vinegar." So, be careful not to harm your beneficial insects or the soil health.

Crop Rotation and Companion Planting: Changing where you plant crops each year can prevent pests from becoming a recurrent problem. Additionally, certain plants when grown together can help each other out, deterring pests, improving growth, or enhancing flavor.

Lastly, patience is key when dealing with garden pests. As the old saying goes, "A watched pot never boils." Often, a minor infestation will clear up on its own, especially if you've encouraged a healthy ecosystem in your garden. Don't be too quick to intervene; sometimes, nature will find its own balance.

CHAPTER 5: COMPOSTING AND RECYCLING.

Alright, now we're getting into the grit of things, as composting is nothing less than the black gold of the garden. So, pull up a chair, and let's get into it.

Introduction "Take care of the land, and the land will take care of you" – there's a heap of wisdom in that old saying. Composting and recycling are part of taking care of the land, turning what could be waste into wealth and closing the circle of life on your homestead.

SECTION 1: THE BASICS OF COMPOSTING

Composting is nature's way of recycling. It's the process of breaking down organic material into a nutrient-rich soil conditioner. But it ain't magic, though sometimes it feels like it might be. It's simply the work of millions of tiny organisms, like bacteria and fungi, that munch away on your leftovers and turn them into something plants can use.

There are a few types of composting you might consider. There's hot composting, where you build a big pile all at once and let it cook, and then there's cold composting, where you add to the pile over time. There's even vermicomposting, where you enlist the help of worms, but we'll talk more about that later.

The golden rule of composting is this – "If it lived once, it can live again." That's to say, if it came from a plant or animal, it can be composted. Veggie scraps, coffee grounds, eggshells, leaves, grass clippings – all these can be composted. However, steer clear of meats, dairy, and diseased plants. Those can attract pests and create unpleasant smells.

SECTION 2: STARTING YOUR COMPOST PILE

Building a compost pile ain't no more difficult than stacking firewood. You'll want to have a mix of 'greens' for nitrogen – like vegetable scraps, coffee grounds, and fresh grass clippings – and 'browns' for carbon – like dried leaves, straw, and shredded paper. Having a good mix is crucial. Too many greens, and your pile might start to smell. Too many browns, and the composting process will slow down. A good ratio to aim for is 3 parts browns to 1-part greens.

Start your pile on bare ground to allow worms and other beneficial organisms to get to it. You can enclose it with a few pallets or a circle of wire fencing to keep it tidy. Layer your materials, starting with a layer of browns, then a layer of greens, and then a layer of garden soil or finished compost to introduce those helpful organisms.

Turn your pile every few weeks to get air in there. This helps speed up the composting process and keeps smells at bay. Add water if it gets too dry, but be careful not to make it soggy. Your compost pile should be as moist as a wrung-out sponge.

Remember, composting is a bit like baking a cake – it needs the right ingredients, a little mixing, and time to 'bake'. Don't get disheartened if it takes a while to get your 'recipe' right. As my granny used to say, "Patience is a virtue, and good compost is worth waiting for."

SECTION 3: VERMICULTURE – COMPOSTING WITH WORMS

Now, for those of you thinking about stepping into the exciting world of worm wrangling, let me tell you - it's a fine choice. Vermiculture, or composting with worms, is a great way to speed up the composting process, especially if you're short on space. These little wrigglers can turn your kitchen scraps into rich, fertile worm castings, which are akin to black gold for your garden, in no time flat.

Getting started with vermicomposting is as easy as pie. You'll need a worm bin, which you can purchase or make yourself out of a couple of plastic storage totes. You'll also need bedding for the worms - moistened, shredded newspaper works well. And of course, you'll need worms. Red wigglers are the best choice for worm bins. Don't just dig up any old earthworms from your yard - they ain't cut out for life in a bin.

Feed your worms a balanced diet of fruit and veggie scraps, coffee grounds, and eggshells. Avoid feeding them citrus, onions, and spicy foods - worms have delicate palates. Also, avoid meat and dairy, which can smell something awful as they decompose.

Remember, "The early bird gets the worm, but the second mouse gets the cheese." In other words, sometimes the best solutions require thinking outside the box. Or in this case, thinking inside the worm bin.

SECTION 4: THE BENEFITS OF COMPOST

Now let's talk about why compost is worth all this effort. Using compost in your garden is like giving your plants a gourmet meal. It improves soil structure, making it easier for roots to grow and water to drain. It adds nutrients that plants need to thrive and can even suppress plant diseases.

Compost also helps soil hold onto moisture, meaning you won't have to water as often. In the scorching heat of summer, that's no small blessing. And it's not just plants that love compost - earthworms and beneficial soil microbes do too. Healthy soil teems with life, and compost helps make that happen.

Plus, making compost is an excellent way to reduce your contribution to the landfill. Kitchen scraps, yard waste, even cardboard and paper - all this can be composted instead of tossed. Just as my pappy used to say, "Waste not, want not." Composting turns what would be waste into something valuable. It's a win-win, for you and for the good ol' Earth.

SECTION 5: RECYCLING ON THE HOMESTEAD

On a homestead, recycling is not just a chore – it's an art form. It's about looking at things not for what they are, but for what they could be. As homesteaders, we're not just stewards of the land, but of all the resources that come our way. The old saying, "One man's trash is another man's treasure," well, that's just daily life on the homestead.

Consider those old wooden pallets that are just lying around. Don't see them as junk. See them as an opportunity. With a bit of elbow grease, those pallets could become a compost bin, a raised bed, or even a rustic piece of outdoor furniture.

Then there are your used coffee grounds. You could toss 'em, sure. But did you know that these little brown gems make a fine natural slug and snail deterrent? That's right. Sprinkle them around your plants, and you've got yourself an eco-friendly pest control solution. Plus, they add nitrogen to your soil – a win-win situation.

Don't overlook those stacks of old newspapers, either. They might seem like yesterday's news, but they're far from useless. Lay them down as a weed-suppressing mulch in your garden or shred them for use in your worm bin or compost pile.

You see, the thing about homesteading is that it cultivates a mindset of resourcefulness. We see value where others see waste, potential where others see problems. It's not just about saving money, although that's certainly a bonus. It's about respecting the cycles of nature, minimizing our footprint on this beautiful planet, and living in harmony with the land.

So, remember to keep an eye out for those treasures in disguise. You never know when or where you'll find the next valuable addition to your homestead.

CHAPTER 6: THE BOUNTY OF YOUR GARDEN

Just as the old saying goes, "The best time to plant a tree was 20 years ago. The second best time is now."

This chapter will guide you on planting the bounty of your homestead: fruits, vegetables, grains, and herbs. All of these hold unique importance and value in a self-reliant lifestyle.

SECTION 1: SOWING YOUR VEGETABLE GARDEN

Let's start by acknowledging that growing vegetables is a labor of love. From the tiny seed that springs forth to the last harvest of the season, there's something downright magical about it. Just remember what my granddad always used to say, "Don't judge each day by the harvest you reap but by the seeds that you plant."

- **Tomatoes:** Tomatoes are like the heart of a vegetable garden, ever-beating with bright red life. There are varieties suited for any climate, from the sun-drenched 'Sun Gold' to the cold-hardy 'Siberia'. Plant them after the last frost date, and provide stakes or cages for support. Tomatoes need plenty of sun, regular watering, and a watchful eye for pests like hornworms.
- **Cucumbers:** Cucumbers are like the long-distance runners of the garden. Given room to run and climb, these prolific plants will produce a bounty of crisp, refreshing fruits. Plant your cucumbers in warm soil and provide them with a trellis for support. They enjoy full sun and require consistent moisture.
- **Potatoes:** Now, growing potatoes is an experience like none other. As the green shoots reach for the sky, a hidden treasure forms beneath the soil. Potatoes can be planted in early spring, and they prefer loose, well-draining soil. Hill the soil around the plants as they grow, and keep an eye out for potato beetles.
- **Beans:** Beans, like true friends, are easy to grow and always give more than they take. Bush beans are more compact, while pole beans will need some support. Plant them after the danger of frost has passed, in full sun and well-drained soil. Beans also enrich the soil with nitrogen – a true gift to the garden.
- **Peppers:** Peppers are the spice of life in a vegetable garden. From sweet bell peppers to fiery habaneros, they offer a world of flavor. Peppers need warm soil and plenty of sunlight. Start seeds indoors or buy young plants, then transplant them after the last frost date. Keep them well-watered, but not waterlogged.

- **Lettuce:** A lettuce patch is a sight to behold. The tender leaves, with their vibrant greens and reds, are like a living salad bowl. Lettuce can be directly sown in the garden in early spring and fall, as it prefers cooler weather. Provide consistent water and consider using shade cloth in hot weather to prevent bolting.
- **Zucchini:** If you're looking for a crop that's as generous as a good neighbor, look no further than zucchini. These squash plants are famed for their abundant yield. Plant them in mounds of well-draining soil, and give them plenty of space – they like to spread out. Keep them well watered and harvest young for the most tender fruits. Remember, though, zucchini plants are like rabbits — they multiply like crazy! So, unless you're feeding an army, a few plants should do the trick.
- **Kale:** Hardy as an old mule and nutritious as anything, kale is a blessing in any garden. This leafy green thrives in the cooler weather of spring and fall. Directly sow the seeds in the garden and water consistently. Once the plant is established, you can harvest the outer leaves and let the plant continue to produce. It's like the plant that keeps on giving!
- **Carrots:** Growing carrots is like digging for buried treasure. This root crop likes loose, well-draining soil and cool temperatures. Sow the seeds directly in the garden, thin to proper spacing, and keep the soil moist. Carrots are a bit slow to start, but once they get going, they're hard to stop. As the old saying goes, "Slow and steady wins the race."
- **Onions:** Onions might make you cry in the kitchen, but they'll sure make you smile in the garden. Plant sets or seeds in early spring, in rows about a foot apart. Onions like a lot of sun and soil that's rich but not too nitrogen-heavy, which can lead to lots of leaves and not enough bulb. Remember to cure your onions in the sun for a few days after harvest to improve their storage life.
- **Beets:** Beets are like the underdogs of the vegetable garden, often overlooked but full of surprises. These root veggies are not only delicious but also extremely nutritious. Directly sow beet seeds in rich, well-draining soil, and thin the seedlings to give the roots room to grow. You can harvest the greens early for salads, and the roots when they're about the size of a golf ball.

Growing vegetables is more than a pastime. It's a way of life. It requires patience, care, and a fair bit of sweat. But as you watch those tiny seeds transform into a bounty of food, you'll realize the wisdom of another saying from my granddad, "Nature does not hurry, yet everything is accomplished." So take your time, enjoy the journey, and relish the feast that your garden provides.

SECTION 2: THE FRUIT OF YOUR LABOR

Fruit trees are a gift that keeps on giving. Once established, they'll provide food for years to come. We'll cover common fruits for the homestead like apples, pears, peaches, and cherries, and discuss how to plant, care for, and harvest your fruit trees.

- **Apples:** Apples are the comfort food of the fruit tree world. They're versatile, storing well for winter pies and sauces, or eaten fresh right off the tree. But remember, as the old saying goes, "An apple tree is easiest to climb when the branches aren't bare." Meaning, patience is key with apple trees; they can take a few years to start producing, but once they do, you'll be rich in fruit. Choose varieties that are disease-resistant and suited to your climate. Trees need to be pruned annually for shape and health.
- **Pears:** Pears are like the quiet, sweet cousin to the apple. A well-tended pear tree can be a thing of beauty and bounty. Like apples, pears need some attention in their early years but will reward you with fruit for decades. Remember to pick pears when they're still a little hard—they ripen from the inside out and will get mushy if left on the tree too long.
- **Peaches:** Now, if you want a taste of sunshine in your hand, you plant yourself a peach tree. These trees like it warm and sunny, but they also need a good chill in the winter. They're a bit fussier than apples and pears, needing careful pruning and often requiring protection from pests and diseases. But the reward is worth it, believe me. As the saying goes, "Life is peachy when you're picking peaches."
- **Cherries:** Cherries are like nature's candy and can bring joy and a little shade to your homestead. You have two basic choices: sweet or sour. Sweet cherries are wonderful for eating fresh, while sour cherries are better for baking. Cherry trees do need some care in the form of pruning and protection from birds who will be very happy to eat your cherries before you get the chance. But as we often say, "Life is just a bowl of cherries." So, remember to enjoy the fruits of your labor.
- **Plums:** Plums are the wild child of the orchard, hearty and relatively easy to grow with varieties suited to many climates. From the sweet juicy European types to the slightly tart Japanese variety, there's a plum to suit every palate. Plums can be eaten fresh, made into preserves, or dried into prunes. But watch out for the fallen fruits—they can be a bit of a slipping hazard.
- **Fig:** Figs, oh the wonderful fig! Talk about a dual-purpose plant. Not only do these trees give us the succulent fig fruit, but they're also a beautiful addition to the landscape. They like it warm, but there are cold-hardy varieties available. Give 'em plenty of sun and a well-draining soil, and they'll be as happy as a pig in mud.

Remember to let figs ripen on the tree for the sweetest fruit. And as we say, "Patience is bitter, but its fruit is sweet."

- **Walnuts:** Walnuts are a mighty tree, strong and tall, providing both shade and sustenance. They prefer deep, well-drained soil and need plenty of space to stretch out. You may not get nuts for the first few years, but with patience, you'll have more walnuts than you can shake a stick at. Remember, "Every mighty oak was once a nut that stood its ground." So too will your walnut tree stand strong and fruitful.
- **Almonds:** Almond trees are a sight to behold, especially in the spring when they're covered in a cloud of white blossoms. Almonds like it dry and warm and will reward you with a bounty of delicious nuts. Just remember, almond trees are among the earliest to bloom, so they can be susceptible to late frosts. As we often say, "It's the early bird that gets the worm, but the second mouse that gets the cheese."
- **Pecans:** Pecan trees are a true Southern favorite. They love the heat and grow big and tall. They do need plenty of room, but once they're established, you'll have pecans aplenty for pies, candied pecans, or just eating straight from the shell. Just remember, pecan trees are a long-term investment. They may take a few years to start producing, but as we say, "Good things come to those who wait."
- **Hazelnuts (Filberts):** Hazelnuts, or filberts, are an excellent choice for cooler, wetter climates. They're a bit smaller than the other nut trees, making them a good choice if space is limited. Plus, they're self-fertile, meaning you only need one to get a good harvest. A hazelnut in the hand is worth two in the bush, so why not plant a few?

Remember, nut trees require a bit more patience than some other trees, but as my grandpappy used to say, "You reap what you sow." Put in the time and effort now, and you'll be rewarded with bountiful harvests for years to come.

SECTION 3: THE STAFF OF LIFE: GROWING GRAINS

Growing grains can be like wrestling a greased pig - a bit challenging but mighty satisfying when you get the hang of it. Now, grains may seem intimidating, but they're just grasses, and like all grasses, they just need good soil, sun, and a little TLC. Here are a few to get you started:

- **Wheat:** Wheat is the backbone of our bread, pasta, and so much more. There are many types of wheat, but for the homesteader, consider hard red winter wheat. It's planted in the fall, grows a bit, then goes dormant for the winter. Come spring, it springs to life and is usually ready to harvest by early summer. And remember,

as we say around here, "Don't eat your seed corn." Save some of your wheat to plant for next year's crop.
- **Corn:** Corn has been a staple for folks for thousands of years. Sweet corn for summer eating is a treat, but don't forget about dent or field corn, which can be ground into cornmeal for baking or used for livestock feed. Be sure to plant in blocks for good pollination, and remember, "Knee-high by the Fourth of July."
- **Oats:** Oats are another excellent grain for the homestead. They can be used for porridge, granola, or ground into flour. They can also be a great cover crop, helping to improve your soil. As my granny used to say, "Plant in the mud and your crop will be a dud." So, wait for the soil to dry a bit in the spring before sowing.

SECTION 4: HERBAL REMEDIES FROM YOUR GARDEN

We're lucky that Mother Nature has seen fit to give us plants that can help heal our ills. This section will help you to create a garden pharmacy. As my granny used to say, "The doctor of the future will give no medicine but will instruct his patient in the care of the human frame, in diet, and in the cause and prevention of disease."

- **Chamomile:** This little daisy-like flower is a powerhouse. It can be used to calm an upset stomach, relieve stress, and help with sleep. Plant in full sun and well-drained soil.
- **Calendula:** Calendula, or pot marigold, has been used for centuries for its healing properties. The flowers can be used to make a salve for cuts, burns, and rashes. It's an easy-to-grow annual that also happens to be pretty as a peach.
- **Echinacea:** Echinacea is well-known for boosting the immune system. It's a prairie native and quite drought-tolerant once established. Plus, the purple flowers are a magnet for butterflies!
- **Lavender:** Lavender isn't just for its sweet fragrance. It's also used for relaxation and to help with sleep. Plus, it's a bee favorite! Plant it in full sun and well-drained soil.
- **Yarrow:** Yarrow is a hardy perennial with feathery leaves and clusters of flowers. It's been used to stop bleeding and for fever and common cold. Yarrow is a tough plant and can grow in poor, dry soils.

Here's a chart of 25 more herbs to consider growing in your backyard pharmacy:

Herb Name	How to Grow	Medicinal Uses
Mint	Prefers rich, moist, and well-drained soil. Grow in full sun or partial shade.	Used for digestive disorders, headaches, and respiratory infections.
Rosemary	Needs well-drained soil and full sun.	Boosts memory, helps with digestion, and has anti-inflammatory compounds.
Thyme	Grows well in well-drained soil and full sun.	Used for respiratory infections, and antiseptic for cuts.
Parsley	Prefers moist, well-drained soil and partial to full sun.	Rich in vitamins, used for kidney health, and boosts immune system.
Dill	Prefers well-drained, slightly acidic soil and full sun.	Can aid in digestion and has antimicrobial effects.
Feverfew	Plant in average, well-drained soil in full sun.	Used for migraines, fever, and arthritis.
Lemon Balm	Grows in rich, moist soil and full sun or part shade.	Used for anxiety, insomnia, and wounds.
Sage	Prefers well-drained, sandy, loamy soil, and full sun.	Helps with digestive problems, menstrual cycle regulation, and has antimicrobial properties.
St. John's Wort	Grows in dry to medium moisture, well-drained soil in full sun.	Used for mild to moderate depression, wounds, and burns.
Ginger	Prefers rich, moist soil and filtered sunlight.	Can help with nausea, reduce inflammation, and improve digestion.
Garlic	Grows well in well-drained, fertile soil and full sun.	Supports immune system, reduces blood pressure, and has antimicrobial properties.
Basil	Prefers rich, well-drained soil and full sun.	Helps with digestion and has anti-inflammatory properties.
Oregano	Plant in well-drained soil and full sun.	Used for respiratory disorders, gastrointestinal disorders, and urinary tract disorders.
Fennel	Prefers rich, well-drained soil and full sun.	Can help with digestion, treat bloating, and increase milk supply in nursing mothers.
Cilantro	Grows well in cool weather, well-drained soil, and full sun to light shade.	Can help with digestion, and has antioxidant, and anti-inflammatory properties.
Valerian	Prefers rich, heavy loam and full sun to partial shade.	Helps with insomnia and anxiety.
Marshmallow	Prefers moist, well-drained soil and full sun to partial shade.	Soothes irritation of mucous membranes, skin, and throat.
Peppermint	Grows in moist, well-drained soil and full sun to partial shade.	Aids in digestion and can relieve headache.
Borage	Plant in rich, well-drained soil and full sun.	Used for adrenal support, eases inflammation, and improves skin health.

Herb Name	How to Grow	Medicinal Uses
Horseradish	Prefers deep, well-drained loamy soil and full sun.	Used for urinary tract infections, kidney stones, fluid retention, and coughs.
Comfrey	Plant in rich, well-drained soil and full sun to partial shade.	Helps in healing wounds, reducing inflammation, and aiding in cell growth.
Ginseng	Grows best in cool, well-drained soil and shaded areas.	Boosts energy, lowers blood sugar and cholesterol levels, reduces stress, and promotes relaxation.
Mullein	Grows in a wide range of soils, including dry, rocky soil. Prefers full sun.	Used for cough, respiratory problems, and earache.
Tansy	Prefers average, well-drained soil and full sun.	Can be used for digestive issues, and to repel insects.
Plantain	Grows in most soils, including poor ones, and either sun or shade.	Can help with skin healing, insect bites, and acts as a mild anti-inflammatory.

CHAPTER 7: LIVESTOCK, POULTRY AND OTHER CRITTERS

SECTION 1: CHOOSING THE RIGHT LIVESTOCK FOR YOUR HOMESTEAD

Picking the right livestock for your homestead isn't a decision to be taken lightly. Just as with selecting the right plot of land, you need to consider a variety of factors and how they align with your goals, capabilities, and resources. So saddle up, and let's explore the process.

1. Assess Your Homestead Size: The size of your homestead largely determines what kind of animals you can keep. Larger animals like cows and horses need more space to roam, while smaller animals like chickens, rabbits, and goats can be raised on smaller plots. If your land is less than an acre, you might want to stick to smaller animals. If you've got a good stretch of green, you could consider larger livestock.

2. Define Your Goals: What do you hope to achieve by raising livestock? Are you looking for a fresh supply of milk, eggs, or meat? Or perhaps you're more interested in their potential to help with tasks around the homestead - like goats for clearing vegetation or chickens for pest control. Maybe it's the companionship of animals you're after. Defining your goals will help you choose livestock that best serve your needs.

3. Consider the Animals' Needs: Each type of livestock has its own specific needs in terms of shelter, feed, care, and social interaction. Dairy animals, for example, need to be milked regularly, which is a significant time commitment. Some animals are more susceptible to certain diseases and require preventative care. Others, like sheep and goats, are social creatures and thrive in a herd. Make sure you fully understand the needs of any animal before you decide to raise it.

4. Suitability for Your Climate and Geography: Not all animals are suited to all environments. For example, certain breeds of cattle do well in hot climates, while others prefer cooler temperatures. Some animals, like goats, prefer hilly terrain, while pigs are happy as a clam in muck and mud. Consider your local climate and geography, and choose animals that are likely to thrive there.

5. Your Time and Resources: Raising livestock takes time and resources. You'll need to feed and water them daily, provide medical care, and keep their living spaces clean. Some animals also require regular grooming or milking. And remember, you'll need to make arrangements for their care if you're away. Make sure you have the time, energy, and resources to devote to raising livestock.

Choosing the right livestock for your homestead is a bit like picking a partner for a square dance. You want someone who's going to keep up with you, match your pace, and make the dance more enjoyable. So, take your time, do your research, and choose animals that will be a good fit for you and your homestead.

SECTION 2: LIVESTOCK AND POULTRY TO CONSIDER

Raising livestock and poultry can be one of the most rewarding aspects of homesteading, but also one of the most demanding. So, whether you're looking to start a small brood of chickens or a full-fledged dairy operation, let's dive deeper into the different types of animals you might consider for your homestead.

1. Cows: Cows can provide a lot of benefits to a homestead. They can produce milk, cheese, butter, and meat, and their manure can enrich your soil. However, they require a lot of space, feed, and care. Dairy cows, in particular, need to be milked twice a day. Cows are social creatures and do best in a herd, so consider having more than one if your land and resources allow.

2. Goats: Goats are a great choice for smaller homesteads. They're smaller than cows but can still provide milk, cheese, and meat. Goats are known for their ability to graze on rough vegetation, which can be helpful for clearing land. They're also known for their escape artistry, so strong, secure fencing is a must.

3. Pigs: Pigs are intelligent, social animals that can provide a significant amount of meat. They require less space than cows but still need plenty of room to root around. Pigs are also great for turning over soil and can help prepare land for planting.

4. Chickens: Chickens are one of the most common choices for homesteaders. They provide eggs, meat, and natural pest control, and their manure is excellent for composting. Chickens require a secure coop and run to protect them from predators, and they need to be fed and watered daily.

5. Ducks: Ducks are another good option for poultry. They're hardy, produce rich, flavorful eggs, and their love of slugs and snails can help keep your garden pest-free. Ducks need a water source for bathing, and like chickens, they need protection from predators.

6. Turkeys: Turkeys can be a little more challenging to raise than chickens or ducks, but they're a popular choice for homesteaders interested in meat production. They require more space and feed than chickens, but their larger size means more meat per bird.

7. Rabbits: Rabbits are a great choice for small homesteads or urban homesteaders. They're small, quiet, and reproduce quickly, providing a sustainable source of lean meat. Their manure can also be directly applied to gardens without composting.

Below is a chart of the top 25 animals to consider for your homestead along with the pros and cons of each:

Animal	Pros	Cons
1. Chicken	Easy to raise, provides eggs and meat, pest control, great for composting.	Susceptible to predators, some breeds can be noisy.
2. Duck	Hardy, provides eggs and meat, good for slug control.	Needs a water source, messy, can be noisy.
3. Turkey	Provides a large amount of meat, can free-range.	Requires more space and feed than chickens, can be harder to raise.
4. Quail	Small size is good for small spaces, fast maturing, provides eggs and meat.	More delicate than chickens, need specialized quail feed.
5. Rabbit	Provides lean meat, quiet, excellent for small spaces.	Not a big egg or milk producer, some people are uncomfortable with the idea of raising rabbits for meat.
6. Goat	Provides milk, cheese, meat, can clear rough vegetation.	Requires secure fencing, can be noisy, susceptible to parasites.
7. Sheep	Provides wool, milk, meat, can graze on pasture.	Requires more space, susceptible to parasites, can be difficult to handle for shearing.
8. Cow	Provides a lot of milk and meat, can work land.	Requires a lot of space and feed, needs regular milking (dairy cows), handling can be difficult.
9. Pig	Provides a lot of meat, good for tilling soil.	Requires substantial feed, can be destructive to land, not the best choice for small spaces.
10. Bee	Provides honey, wax, and pollination services.	Can sting, needs regular inspections and management, honey extraction equipment can be expensive.
11. Alpaca	Provides fiber, can be used for trekking, relatively low maintenance.	Requires special fencing, needs companionship, shearing can be a challenge.
12. Guinea Fowl	Excellent pest control, particularly ticks, can provide meat.	Very noisy, tends to roam, not as prolific egg layers as chickens.

Animal	Pros	Cons
13. Donkey	Can provide protection for other livestock, can work land.	Can be stubborn, requires a lot of space, needs regular hoof care.
14. Horse	Can work land, potential for riding, manure is great for composting.	Requires a lot of space and feed, needs regular hoof and vet care, can be expensive to maintain.
15. Llama	Provides fiber, can guard other livestock, relatively low maintenance.	Needs companionship, shearing can be a challenge, can spit when threatened.
16. Geese	Can provide meat and eggs, excellent at weed control, can act as 'watchdogs'.	Can be aggressive, noisy, needs a water source.
17. Pigeon	Provides meat, can be used for show or racing.	Requires specific housing and care, not a big meat producer, can attract predators.
18. Catfish (aquaponics)	Provides meat, good for water gardening system.	Needs specific equipment, must monitor water conditions, not suitable for all climates.
19. Earthworms (vermiculture)	Produces rich compost, can sell worms for bait.	Requires management of bin, not a direct food source.
20. Muscovy Duck	Provides meat and eggs, good insect control, less noisy than other ducks.	Needs a water source, can be broody, slower to mature than chickens.
21. Mule	Can work land, more hardy than horses.	Sterile (cannot reproduce), needs a lot of space and regular hoof care.
22. Deer (game farming)	Provides venison, potential for tourism (deer watching).	Requires a lot of space and secure fencing, needs licensing in many areas, shy animals.
23. Buffalo	Provides meat, potential for tourism.	Requires a lot of space and secure fencing, can be challenging to handle, not suitable for small homesteads.
24. Emu	Provides meat, eggs, and oil, can be used for tourism.	Requires a lot of space and secure fencing, can be challenging to handle, not suitable for small homesteads.
25. Silkworms	Provides silk, relatively easy to raise.	Requires a constant supply of mulberry leaves, not a direct food source.

SECTION 3: UNDERSTANDING THE LAWS PERTAINING TO LIVESTOCK AND POULTRY

Legal matters might not be the most exciting aspect of homesteading, but they're a critical part of planning and establishing your farm. As the old saying goes, "An ounce of prevention is worth a pound of cure."

Every country, state, and even local municipality can have different laws when it comes to livestock and poultry. These laws can dictate what types of animals you're allowed to raise, how many you can keep, and how they must be housed and cared for.

Start with your local zoning laws. These can often be found on your city or county's website, or by calling your local government office. In many residential areas, there may be restrictions on raising certain types of livestock, particularly larger animals like cows or pigs. Even chickens aren't allowed in some places, or there may be a limit to the number you can have.

Animal welfare laws are another important consideration. These laws are designed to ensure that animals are treated humanely and live in acceptable conditions. Make sure you fully understand the requirements for space, shelter, food and water, and general care for each type of animal you intend to keep.

Keep in mind that selling animal products, like meat, milk, or eggs, may involve yet another set of regulations, including food safety and business licensing requirements.

SECTION 4: CARING FOR YOUR ANIMALS

Raising animals is a big responsibility. Each type of animal has specific needs and requires care and attention to thrive. As my grandpappy used to say, "Treat your animals well, and they'll do the same for you."

Feeding your animals is one of the most important aspects of their care. Each type of animal has specific dietary needs. For example, chickens need a diet rich in protein, while goats need a balanced diet that includes plenty of roughage. Some animals can graze and forage for much of their food, while others will rely more heavily on feed you provide.

Routine health check-ups are a crucial part of animal care. Regular inspections will help you catch any potential issues early, before they become serious problems. Look out for signs of common health issues such as parasites, respiratory problems, or foot issues.

Creating a suitable living environment for each type of animal is also essential. Animals need shelter from the elements, enough space to move around comfortably, and a clean, healthy environment to prevent disease. Think about fencing for animals that graze, nesting boxes for chickens, and sturdy, warm shelters for all.

Remember, the key to good animal care is attentiveness. Pay attention to your animals, get to know their normal behaviors and sounds, and you'll quickly notice if something's amiss. As any old farmer will tell you, "An ounce of observation is worth a pound of vet bills."

SECTION 5: BEES, WORMS AND OTHER CRITTERS

There's a lot more to a thriving homestead than large livestock and poultry. A host of smaller creatures can bring great benefits, too. Let's delve into some of these, starting with the buzzing world of bees.

Beekeeping: Bees are remarkable creatures. Not only do they provide sweet honey and beeswax, but they also play a crucial role in pollinating your garden and fruit trees. Getting started in beekeeping requires some specific equipment such as a bee suit, hive boxes, a smoker, and of course, the bees themselves. It's also advisable to educate yourself on bee behavior, hive management, and potential challenges like mites or disease. Many communities have local beekeeping clubs where you can learn from experienced beekeepers and even source your initial bees.

Beekeeping requires regular checks on the hive, but it's relatively low-labor compared to the care required for larger livestock. Just remember the old beekeeper's saying, "A swarm in May is worth a load of hay; a swarm in June is worth a silver spoon; but a swarm in July is not worth a fly." Essentially, start early in the season for the best results.

Vermiculture: Earthworms might not be as glamorous as bees, but they can be a homesteader's best friend. By consuming organic waste, these little wrigglers produce worm castings, a form of compost that's rich in nutrients. A worm bin is relatively easy to set up and maintain, and it can help you recycle kitchen scraps while improving your garden's soil.

Aquaculture: Raising fish, such as tilapia or catfish, can be a valuable addition to a homestead, providing a source of protein that requires less space than most livestock. It's possible to raise fish in a backyard pond, or even integrate fish farming with gardening through a method known as aquaponics. In an aquaponics system, fish and plants are grown together in a mutually beneficial cycle. The fish produce waste, which serves as organic food for the plants. In return, the plants naturally filter the water, which is recirculated back to the fish.

Before diving into aquaculture or aquaponics, research your local regulations and the specific needs of the fish species you're interested in. Also, consider the setup and maintenance costs of an aquaculture system.

Remember, whether you're drawn to the sweet rewards of beekeeping, the soil-enhancing benefits of vermiculture, or the dual-purpose efficiency of aquaponics, these smaller-scale ventures can add considerable value to your homestead.

CHAPTER 8: HARVESTING & PRESERVING

The moment of harvest is when all your hard work comes to fruition. But harvesting is just the beginning – how you preserve your bounty will dictate the quality of your homegrown produce and the diversity of your diet throughout the year.

This chapter will guide you through the harvesting process and various preservation techniques, ensuring you get the most out of your hard-earned harvest.

SECTION 1: HOW TO PROPERLY HARVEST YOUR PRODUCE

Harvesting is more than just reaping what you've sown - it's an art that requires knowledge and timing. Recognizing the right moment to harvest ensures that your fruits, vegetables, grains, and herbs have reached peak flavor, nutrition, and appropriate condition for preserving.

- **Signs of Ripeness**: The first step to successful harvesting is recognizing when your produce is ripe. While this varies across different types of fruits, vegetables, and grains, there are some common signs to look out for. This includes color changes (for instance, tomatoes turning a deep red), a particular size or shape, a distinct aroma, or a change in texture. For grains like wheat and corn, the kernels should be hard and dry. For root vegetables like potatoes and carrots, the tops often die back when the roots are ready.
- **Harvesting Techniques**: The method of harvesting varies by plant type. Some produce, such as tomatoes and peppers, can be gently twisted off the vine, while others, like carrots and potatoes, need to be carefully unearthed. For leafy greens, it's often best to pick leaves from the outside, allowing the center to continue growing. Grains such as wheat and corn should be cut close to the base. In all cases, aim to avoid damage to the plant or the produce itself.
- **Storing Your Harvest**: Correct storage can greatly extend the life of your harvest. Cool, dry, dark places are often best for many vegetables and grains, while some fruits do well in a warmer area. Potatoes, onions, and garlic, for example, store well in a cool, dark pantry, while apples need a cool but not freezing space like a cellar or fridge. Some produce, such as tomatoes and bananas, emit ethylene gas which can hasten ripening (and over-ripening) of other fruits and vegetables, so they should be stored separately.
- **Seed Saving**: As you harvest, consider saving seeds from your best plants for next year's crops. For tomatoes, cucumbers, and peppers, the seeds need to be cleaned and dried before storage. For beans and peas, let the pods dry on the vine before harvesting

the seeds. In all cases, ensure seeds are thoroughly dried before storing them in a cool, dark place.

Remember the wise words of Robert Louis Stevenson: "Don't judge each day by the harvest you reap but by the seeds that you plant." Harvesting is not only the culmination of one season's work; it's also the first step in preparing for the next season.

SECTION 2: OVERVIEW OF CANNING AND PRESERVING

Just like planting a seed or nurturing an animal, preserving food is an important part of the homesteading journey. It's a way to capture the bounty of your harvest and enjoy it throughout the year. This section will introduce the basics of preserving food, with a focus on canning, and will also touch on pickling and fermenting.

Water Bath Canning vs. Pressure Canning: There are two primary methods of canning - water bath canning and pressure canning. The method you choose depends on the acidity of the food you are canning. High-acid foods like fruits, jams, jellies, pickles, and tomatoes with added acid can be processed in a boiling water bath. Low-acid foods like vegetables, meats, and poultry need to be canned using a pressure canner, which achieves higher temperatures needed to destroy harmful bacteria and botulism spores.

Equipment: The essential equipment for canning includes glass jars with two-part lids (a flat lid with a rubber gasket and a screw-on band), a large pot for water bath canning or a pressure canner, a jar lifter, and a funnel.

Safety Procedures: Safety is paramount when it comes to canning. Always use recipes from trusted sources that have been tested for safety. Inspect your jars and lids for any cracks or defects. Ensure your preserved foods are properly sealed and stored in a cool, dark place. And always check for signs of spoilage before consuming canned goods, including foul odors, leaking or bulging lids, and any unusual color or texture.

Pickling and Fermenting: Beyond canning, there are other methods of preservation that you may want to explore. Pickling involves preserving foods in an acidic solution, usually vinegar, and can be used for a variety of vegetables. Fermenting, on the other hand, involves preserving food through the process of lacto-fermentation, which can provide added health benefits such as probiotics. Foods commonly fermented include cabbage (to make sauerkraut or kimchi), cucumbers, and various other vegetables and fruits.

As the old saying goes, "Preserving the harvest is preserving the work of our hands and the gifts of the earth." Embracing the art of preserving not only allows you to enjoy your harvest year-round but also ties you to the generations of farmers and homesteaders who have used these methods to sustain their families and communities throughout the seasons.

SECTION 3: PRESERVING MEATS AND DAIRY

Raising livestock for meat and dairy is a significant step in your homesteading journey. Once you've taken this step, the next is learning how to safely preserve these products. From smoking and curing meat to turning milk into cheese, this section will guide you through the processes that allow you to enjoy your home-raised products year-round.

Preserving Meats: When it comes to meat, freshness is key, but so is understanding how to safely store and preserve your bounty. Here are some of the common methods for preserving meats:

- **Smoking**: This method uses the smoke from wood chips to both flavor and preserve the meat. It can be done in a smoker or even a grill. Meat should be cured before smoking for safety.
- **Curing**: This involves applying a mixture of salt, sugar, and curing salt to the meat, then allowing it to sit in this mixture for a certain period. The curing process draws moisture from the meat, slowing down the growth of spoilage-causing bacteria.
- **Jerky**: Making jerky involves slicing meat into thin strips, marinating it in a mixture of your choice, then drying it at low heat until it is fully dehydrated.
- **Canning**: Meat can be preserved through canning, which involves packing the meat into jars and processing it in a pressure canner. This method allows for long-term storage at room temperature.
- **Freezing**: Freezing is a simple and effective way to preserve meat, though it requires a lot of freezer space. It's important to wrap meat properly or vacuum seal it to prevent freezer burn.

Preserving Dairy: If you're raising cows or goats, you'll likely find yourself with a surplus of milk at times. Here's how you can preserve it:

- **Cheese**: Making cheese is a traditional way of preserving excess milk. It can be as simple as making cottage cheese or as complex as aged hard cheese.

- **Yogurt**: Making yogurt is another excellent way to preserve milk. It requires heating the milk, adding a yogurt culture, and keeping it at a steady warm temperature to ferment.
- **Butter**: Churning cream separates it into butter and buttermilk, both of which can be used in a variety of ways in your kitchen.

As the saying goes, "Good meat and good cheese need good care." Understanding the basics of preserving meats and dairy can help ensure that the fruits of your labor are enjoyed to their fullest.

SECTION 4: PRESERVING FRUITS AND VEGETABLES

Preserving fruits and vegetables harvested from your homestead garden allows you to capture their freshness and enjoy them throughout the year. There are many different ways to preserve these treasures of your garden, each with its benefits and ideal uses.

- **Canning**: Canning is a great way to store a variety of fruits and vegetables. From canned tomatoes for your sauces to peaches in syrup for a winter treat, the options are endless. This process involves placing the produce in jars with either water, syrup, or juice and heating them to kill any microorganisms. It's important to remember that low-acid vegetables, like green beans or corn, need to be pressure canned for safety reasons, while high-acid fruits like berries and apples can be safely canned in a water bath.
- **Freezing**: Freezing fruits and vegetables is one of the easiest ways to preserve them. Many vegetables should be blanched first to help maintain their quality. Berries can be frozen on trays and then packed into bags to prevent them from sticking together.
- **Drying**: Drying is an ancient preservation method that's especially good for fruits. Apples, pears, peaches, and berries can all be dried and used in baking, cooking, or just as a snack. Vegetables like tomatoes, peppers, and beans can also be dried. You can use a dehydrator, an oven on a low setting, or even sun drying for some fruits in very hot climates.
- **Jams and Jellies**: Making jam or jelly is a popular way to preserve many types of fruit. The process involves cooking the fruit with sugar and pectin until it gels. These sweet spreads are a delight on homemade bread.
- **Relishes and Salsas**: A tasty way to preserve a variety of vegetables and some fruits is by making relishes or salsas. These can add a flavor punch to meals throughout the year.

Each method has its best uses, depending on the type of produce and how you want to use it later. As a homesteader, you have the privilege of choosing the right method to suit your needs and tastes. Remember, the goal of preserving is to maintain as much of the original flavor and nutritional value as possible, so always start with the freshest produce and handle it carefully.

Keep in mind that "What we preserve today, we can savor tomorrow." Enjoy the fruits of your labor all year round and remember that each jar opened in the middle of winter is a taste of summer's sunshine.

CHAPTER 9: DAILY PRODUCTION & BEEKEEPING

Homesteading provides many opportunities for self-sufficiency, and two of the most rewarding are dairy production and beekeeping. This chapter will guide you through the steps of handling and processing dairy, understanding the fundamentals of beekeeping, and creatively using dairy and honey in your homemade recipes. As the saying goes, "Bread and honey feed the body, milk and honey soothe the soul."

SECTION 1: HOW TO HANDLE AND PROCESS DAIRY

Dairy production is an exciting and rewarding aspect of homesteading. It provides an abundant source of nourishment for your family and the satisfaction that comes from producing your own food. Whether it's from cows or goats, fresh milk is a versatile commodity that can be processed into a variety of tasty and nutritious products. But let's not put the cart before the horse. Before you can enjoy that delicious homemade cheese or glass of fresh, cold milk, there are steps to be taken to ensure the health of your animals, the quality of your milk, and the safety of your dairy products.

1. Milking the Animals: The first step to getting that coveted milk is to milk your cows or goats. For cows, milking should typically be done twice a day, usually early morning and late afternoon. Goats can also be milked twice a day, although some goat breeds only require once a day milking. Always ensure your hands, the milking area, and equipment are clean. Calm and gentle handling during milking contributes to better milk let-down and a more efficient process.

2. Handling and Storing Milk: Once the milk is collected, it needs to be filtered and chilled quickly. This helps to keep the milk fresh and slow down the growth of bacteria. To do this, first filter the milk to remove any impurities, using a fine mesh strainer or a special milk filter. Then, promptly place it in a refrigerator set at below 40 degrees Fahrenheit (4 degrees Celsius).

3. Pasteurizing Milk: You might choose to pasteurize your milk to kill any potential harmful bacteria. Pasteurization involves heating the milk to a specific temperature for a set period of time and then quickly cooling it. This process doesn't significantly affect the milk's nutritional content and can make it safer, especially for children or people with compromised immune systems.

4. Making Dairy Products: If you've ever wanted to try your hand at making your own dairy products, homesteading provides the perfect opportunity. With fresh milk, you can make butter, cheese, and yogurt right in your own kitchen.

- **Butter:** Making butter involves agitating cream (which you can collect from your fresh milk) until it forms a solid. This process can be done with a butter churner or even a jar with a tight-fitting lid.
- **Cheese:** Cheese is made by adding a starter culture to milk to change the lactose into lactic acid, then adding an enzyme called rennet to coagulate the milk into curds and whey. The curds are then cut, cooked, drained, and pressed into cheese.
- **Yogurt:** Yogurt is made by heating milk, then adding a yogurt starter culture, and keeping the mixture at a consistent temperature until it thickens and develops the tangy flavor characteristic of yogurt.

5. Cleanliness and Hygiene: Remember, the quality and safety of your milk and dairy products rely heavily on cleanliness and good hygiene practices. Ensure your milking equipment, containers, and any utensils used in processing your milk are thoroughly cleaned and sterilized.

Remember, "A quart of milk a day keeps the doctor away." The benefits of raising dairy animals extend far beyond just the daily fresh milk. They provide companionship, contribute to sustainable living, and provide nutrient-rich manure for your gardens. Now, go enjoy that glass of milk or slab of cheese, and give yourself a pat on the back for a job well done!

SECTION 2: RAISING CHICKENS AND HARVESTING EGGS

Having a flock of chickens on your homestead offers numerous benefits, from their excellent bug control to their high-quality manure, perfect for composting. But perhaps the most delightful benefit is fresh eggs. However, to make sure your chickens are happy, healthy, and productive layers, there are some key things you need to know. Remember, as they say, "The key to everything is patience. You get the chicken by hatching the egg, not by smashing it."

1. Understanding Chicken Breeds and Egg Production: Firstly, not all chickens are created equal when it comes to laying eggs. Some breeds are known for their exceptional egg production, like White Leghorns, Rhode Island Reds, and Sussex chickens. These breeds can lay between 200 to 300 eggs per year, depending on their environment and care.

2. Providing Optimal Living Conditions: The quality of your chickens' environment can greatly affect their egg production. Chickens need a safe, spacious coop that protects them from predators and harsh weather conditions. Each chicken needs about 2-3 square feet inside the coop and 8-10 square feet in an outdoor run.

Ventilation is important to prevent respiratory diseases, but drafts should be avoided in the colder months. Roosting bars for sleeping and nesting boxes for laying are also essential. Typically, you'll need one nesting box for every 3-4 hens.

3. Proper Nutrition: Nutrition plays a key role in egg production. Layers need a balanced diet rich in protein and calcium. You can buy commercial layer feeds that meet these nutritional requirements. Offering a calcium supplement like oyster shell in a separate dish allows hens to take what they need for strong eggshells.

4. Increasing Egg Production: Light is a significant factor in egg production. Hens require 14-16 hours of daylight to lay regularly. In winter months, when daylight hours shorten, egg production can naturally drop off. Some keepers choose to add supplemental light in the coop to maintain production, but it's also fine to let the hens have a rest period.

Consistent stress can decrease egg production. This could be caused by changes in the environment, predators, or bullying among the flock. So, ensure your hens feel secure and happy in their environment.

5. Collecting and Storing Eggs: Eggs should be collected from the nesting boxes at least once a day to prevent them from getting dirty or cracked. After collecting, clean any dirty eggs with a dry cloth. Avoid washing eggs until you're ready to use them, as this can remove the natural protective coating called the 'bloom', which helps to keep bacteria out.

Fresh eggs can be stored at room temperature for several days, but for longer storage, they should be kept in the refrigerator where they can last for several weeks.

Raising chickens for eggs is a rewarding endeavor that gives back in so many ways. So, keep these tips in mind, and you'll be well on your way to a bountiful egg harvest.

SECTION 3: THE BASICS OF BEEKEEPING

Beekeeping, or apiculture, is a fascinating and rewarding endeavor that's not only beneficial for your homestead but also for your local ecosystem. It requires knowledge, patience, and a bit of courage. But as any seasoned beekeeper will tell you, the rewards are worth the effort. As the old saying goes, "Bees work for man, and yet they never bruise their master's flower, but leave it having done, as fair as ever."

1. Understanding Bees and Their Roles: A bee colony is a highly organized society, with various types of bees each performing specific roles. The queen bee is the mother of all bees in the hive; her job is to lay eggs and produce pheromones that guide the hive's activities. The worker bees are females that do not reproduce but perform all the work of the hive - they forage for food, clean and protect the hive, circulate air by beating their wings, and perform many other societal functions. The male bees, or drones, have only one job, and that is to mate with a virgin queen.

2. Beekeeping Equipment: The most common type of hive used in modern beekeeping is the Langstroth hive. It contains stackable boxes filled with frames that provide a place for bees to build their honeycomb.

You'll also need a bee suit to protect you from stings, a smoker to calm the bees during inspections, a hive tool to help you pry apart the sticky frames, and a bee brush to gently remove bees from areas where you don't want them.

3. Getting Bees: You can obtain bees by purchasing a nucleus colony, or "nuc", which is a small, already functioning colony with a queen, worker bees, and brood. Alternatively, you could buy a package of bees, which is a box containing a queen and a certain weight of worker bees, usually 2 or 3 pounds.

4. Inspecting Your Hive: Regular hive inspections will allow you to monitor the health of your bees, check if the queen is laying, look for signs of disease or pests, and assess the honey stores. During these inspections, you should be gentle and slow in your movements to avoid alarming the bees.

5. Dealing with Challenges: Keeping bees isn't without its challenges. Pests like Varroa mites can infest your hives, and diseases like American foulbrood can decimate your colony. Learning how to identify and deal with these challenges is part of becoming a successful beekeeper.

6. Harvesting Your Honey: The moment every beekeeper looks forward to is the honey harvest. This usually happens in late summer or early fall, depending on your local climate and floral resources. Before harvesting, you should ensure that there's enough honey left for the bees to survive the winter.

The honey is extracted from the frames using a special centrifuge called a honey extractor, after which it can be strained and bottled. Remember, honey is a precious gift from your bees and should be appreciated as such.

Beekeeping is a unique and fulfilling aspect of homesteading that brings its own sweet rewards. As the saying goes, "The bee's life is like a magic well: the more you draw from it, the more it fills with water." May your journey into beekeeping be filled with joy and plenty of honey!

CHAPTER 10: OFF THE GRID POWER, WATER & SANITATION

Living off-grid is an ambitious goal that comes with its own set of unique challenges and rewards. This chapter will discuss the essentials for successful off-grid living, covering topics such as power and heating, water management, and waste management. Remember, "To live off the grid requires you to shift your thinking not only about what you need, but what you can do without."

SECTION 1: POWER AND HEATING

Living off the grid necessitates an alternative to traditional utility-based power sources. Let's consider the four most common options: solar power, wind power, hydroelectric power, and biomass.

1. Solar Power: Solar power harnesses energy from the sun's rays to generate electricity. This is usually done using photovoltaic cells assembled into panels.

Pros:

- Renewable and abundant energy source.
- Minimal maintenance required once installed.

Cons:

- Initial installation cost can be high.
- Power generation depends on sunlight, making it less effective in areas with less sun exposure or during winter months.

Implementation Tips:

- Start small by powering a single appliance or outbuilding with solar to get used to the technology before transitioning completely.
- Battery storage is a critical component of your solar setup, ensuring you have power during the night or overcast days.

2. Wind Power: Wind turbines generate power from the wind, converting kinetic energy into mechanical energy, which is then transformed into electrical energy.

Pros:

- A good complement to solar energy in many climates, as it can produce power at night and during cloudy weather.
- A powerful generator if you live in a windy area.

Cons:

- Wind turbines can be noisy and visually intrusive.
- Wind speed can be inconsistent, requiring alternative sources for periods of calm.

Implementation Tips:

- Check average wind speeds in your area before investing to ensure you'll generate sufficient power.
- Consider your neighbors – if you live close to others, the noise could be a disturbance.

3. Hydroelectric Power: This system uses the flow of water, typically a stream or river, to spin a turbine that generates power.

Pros:

- If you have a reliable water source, it can provide consistent, around-the-clock energy.
- Excellent for locations with a high annual rainfall or an on-site river/stream.

Cons:

- Requires specific geographical features that are not available to everyone.
- Potential impact on local aquatic ecosystems.

Implementation Tips:

- You must ensure you have the necessary legal permissions to manipulate waterways on your property.
- Maintenance of your water source and hydroelectric system is critical to ensure consistent operation.

4. Biomass: This involves burning organic material, typically wood or pellets, to provide heat and, in some cases, power through a biomass boiler or stove.

Pros:

- If you have a woodland, biomass can be a very cheap and sustainable heating source.
- Can be used for both heating and cooking.

Cons:

- Requires a significant amount of storage space for the fuel.
- Regular cleaning and maintenance are needed.

Implementation Tips:

- Ensure you have a sustainable and manageable source of fuel before investing.
- Learn about the different types of stoves and boilers to decide which would suit your needs best.

By understanding these alternative power sources, you can make an informed decision about which would work best for your homestead, keeping in mind factors like your local climate, resources, and energy needs. Remember, achieving off-grid living isn't an overnight process but a gradual transition, learning and adapting as you go.

SECTION 2: WATER MANAGEMENT

1. Securing a Water Source:

- **Well Water:** If your property has access to groundwater, digging or drilling a well can be an excellent way to secure a reliable water source. Depending on your location and the depth required, you may need professional assistance. Be sure to get your well water tested to ensure it's safe for consumption.
- **Rainwater Collection:** Rainwater collection systems can range from simple rain barrels under downspouts to more complex systems with storage tanks, filters, and pumps. Be aware that in some areas, collecting rainwater is regulated or even illegal, so it's crucial to check local laws.
- **Surface Water:** If your homestead has a stream, river, or pond, this can also serve as a water source. Keep in mind that surface water will require more intensive filtration and purification before use.

2. Water Purification and Filtration:

No matter where your water comes from, it's essential to purify it to make sure it's safe to drink. Common methods include boiling, using a water filter, chemical purification (iodine or chlorine tablets), or UV sterilization.

More complex filtration systems may be necessary depending on your water source, especially if you're using surface water. These could include ceramic filters, activated charcoal filters, or reverse osmosis systems.

3. Efficient Water Usage:

In an off-grid homestead, it's especially crucial to be conscious of your water usage. Some techniques for water conservation include:

- Using low-flow fixtures and appliances.
- Reusing greywater from sinks and showers for flushing toilets or watering gardens.
- Using drip irrigation in gardens to minimize water waste.
- Regularly checking and repairing any leaks.

SECTION 3: WASTE MANAGEMENT

1. Composting Toilets: Composting toilets are a type of dry toilet that uses the process of decomposition to turn human waste into compost-like material. They're an ideal solution for off-grid living as they require no plumbing or water to function, significantly reducing water usage and waste production.

These toilets come in various designs, but most separate solid and liquid waste to control odor and facilitate composting. After each use, a layer of material like sawdust, coconut coir, or peat moss is added to the solids container to cover waste and help the composting process.

The resulting compost should be handled with care. While it's often safe to use on ornamental plants, it's usually not recommended for edible crops due to potential pathogens.

2. Septic Systems: Septic systems are another solution for waste management on an off-grid homestead. A typical septic system consists of a septic tank and a drain field. Solids settle to the bottom of the tank, where bacteria break them down, while liquids flow out into the drain field, where they are further treated by the soil.

Installing a septic system requires significant upfront investment and usually requires professional installation to ensure it's correctly placed and constructed. Regular maintenance, including pumping out the tank every 3-5 years, is crucial to prevent failures and leaks.

3. Greywater Systems: Greywater systems allow you to reuse waste water from showers, sinks, and washing machines in your garden, saving on water usage and reducing the load on your septic system or composting toilet.

Simple systems might involve a direct line from the washing machine to the garden, while more complex systems could include filters, pumps, and surge tanks. If using greywater, ensure your soaps and detergents are biodegradable and garden-safe.

4. Managing Waste Responsibly: Whatever systems you choose, managing your waste responsibly is a critical part of living off-grid. This not only includes human waste but also kitchen scraps, which can be composted, and trash, which should be minimized and responsibly disposed of.

In summary, effective waste management systems are crucial for preserving the environment, maintaining personal health, and complying with local regulations. As the saying goes, "Waste not, want not." In an off-grid situation, your waste can become a resource, contributing to a self-sufficient and sustainable lifestyle.

SECTION 4: COMMUNICATION AND INTERNET

While living off-grid provides a chance to disconnect and live more intimately with nature, maintaining reliable communication channels is essential for safety, convenience, and remaining connected with the broader world. Let's dive into some options:

1. Satellite Internet: Satellite internet is an excellent option for off-grid living as it can provide coverage virtually anywhere on the planet, regardless of how remote your homestead might be. It operates by sending and receiving signals from a satellite orbiting Earth.

While it provides global coverage, there are a few drawbacks. Weather can sometimes disrupt the service, and latency (delay) can be high due to the long distances signals must travel. It's also typically more expensive and offers less bandwidth compared to wired connections. However, recent advancements in satellite internet technologies are promising, with companies like SpaceX's Starlink aiming to provide high-speed, reliable satellite internet services globally.

2. Mobile Hotspots: If your homestead is within reach of a cellular network, using a mobile hotspot for internet access could be a viable solution. A mobile hotspot uses a smartphone or a dedicated device (like a portable router) to connect to a cellular network, providing a Wi-Fi signal that other devices can connect to.

The downside is that service quality can vary based on the distance from the cell tower, obstructions, and network congestion. Moreover, data plans can be expensive, especially if you require a lot of data.

3. Ham Radio: Amateur or ham radio is a reliable, tried-and-true method of off-grid communication. It doesn't rely on any infrastructure other than your own equipment and can allow you to connect with others over vast distances. It's particularly valuable in emergency situations when other communication networks might be unavailable.

Becoming a ham radio operator requires a license. Studying for your license will provide a deep understanding of how radio works and how to operate your equipment effectively.

4. Other Options: Depending on your location, other options may be available. Traditional landline phones can sometimes be installed in remote locations. Also, certain internet service providers specialize in rural and remote internet access and might have solutions that work for your area.

Lastly, it's essential to remember that in an off-grid situation, emergency communication is vital. Ensure you have a reliable method of contacting help if necessary. As the saying goes, "It's better to be a year early than a minute too late."

CHAPTER 11: ESSENTIAL HOMESTEADING SKILLS

In this chapter, we will delve into the various skills that not only enrich your homesteading experience but can also prove invaluable after a crisis. From spinning and weaving to woodworking and candle making, these skills serve not just practical purposes, but can also become fulfilling hobbies. We will also touch on the importance of building, maintenance, and repair skills. Lastly, we will explore the world of ammo reloading and gunsmithing. Remember, "A man of many trades begs bread never."

SECTION 1: TRADITIONAL HOMESTEADING SKILLS

Embracing a homesteading lifestyle often involves reconnecting with age-old skills that our ancestors relied on for their everyday needs. Mastering these skills not only provides a sense of accomplishment but also yields practical products that can enhance your self-sufficiency.

Spinning and Weaving: Before the advent of mechanized textile production, spinning and weaving were critical skills. If you're raising sheep, alpacas, or other fiber-producing animals, or growing cotton or flax plants, spinning and weaving can transform these raw materials into valuable end products.

- **Spinning:** Spinning is the process of turning raw fiber into yarn or thread. Whether you're using a drop spindle or a spinning wheel, the fundamentals are the same: drafting (pulling the fibers into a thinner strand) and then twisting them to give them strength and cohesion. Spinning requires patience and practice, but with time, you'll find a rhythm that works for you, creating beautiful and unique yarns in the process.
- **Weaving:** Once you have your yarn, weaving transforms it into fabric. At its simplest, weaving involves interlacing two sets of threads – the warp (longitudinal threads attached to the loom) and the weft (transverse threads) – to create cloth.

Woodworking: Woodworking is a valuable skill on the homestead, allowing you to create and repair many of the tools and structures you need.

- **Understanding different types of wood:** This involves knowing the characteristics, strengths, and weaknesses of different wood types, and which are best suited to particular tasks – from construction to furniture-making to carving.
- **Using hand tools and basic joinery techniques**: Learning to use tools like saws, chisels, planes, and drills, and mastering joints like the dovetail, mortise and tenon, and lap joint will equip you to tackle a wide variety of woodworking projects.

Candle Making:

Whether for lighting, ritual, or simply creating a cozy atmosphere, candles have been a staple in homes for centuries.

- **Wax types:** Introduce yourself to the different types of wax you can use – including beeswax, soy wax, and paraffin – and their respective properties and uses.
- **Candle-making process:** From melting the wax and preparing the wick, to pouring the candle and adding color and scent, you should learn the candle-making process, giving you the knowledge and confidence to experiment with your own candle creations.

Soap Making:

Making your own soap can be a rewarding way to have control over the ingredients that go into your skincare products.

- **Understanding saponification:** This is the chemical process that turns fats and lye into soap.
- **Cold process soap-making**: This is the most traditional method of making soap. research instructions and recipes for making your own cold-process soaps, from simple single-oil soaps to more complex and creative formulations.
- **Melt and pour soap-making:** For those not quite ready to work with lye, you can learn how to melt and pour soap-making, where you start with a pre-made soap base that you can then customize with your choice of colors, scents, and additives.

SECTION 2: BUILDING, MAINTENANCE, AND REPAIR SKILLS

As a homesteader, it's likely you'll find yourself undertaking tasks traditionally handled by a variety of skilled tradespeople. From basic carpentry to essential home maintenance, developing these practical skills can greatly benefit your self-sufficient lifestyle.

Basic Carpentry: Carpentry is an invaluable skill for a homesteader, allowing you to build and repair essential structures around your property.

- ***Understanding Wood and Materials:*** Different types of wood have various properties, making them better suited to certain tasks. For example, cedar is naturally resistant to decay and works well for outdoor projects, while pine is affordable and easy to work with for indoor tasks. Beyond wood, understanding how and when to use other materials like screws, nails, and adhesives is important. For instance, screws hold better than nails in many situations, but nails are often faster and easier to install.

- **Tool Knowledge:** Many carpentry tasks can be achieved with a basic set of tools. A hammer, saw, tape measure, square, level, and drill will take care of most jobs. Learn to maintain your tools by cleaning them regularly, keeping them sharp, and storing them properly to extend their lifespan.
- **Basic Construction Techniques:** Start by mastering how to measure and cut accurately, a critical aspect of any carpentry project. Learn to assemble structures using different types of joints, such as butt joints for simplicity or dovetail joints for strength.

Home Maintenance and Repair:

As a homesteader, preventative maintenance can save you from costly repairs down the road. Regularly inspect your home for potential issues, like a leaking roof or cracks in the foundation.

- *Plumbing:* Basic plumbing skills can be a lifesaver. Learn to fix a leaky faucet, unclog drains, and even install new fixtures. While more significant issues may require a professional, many common problems can be addressed with a bit of knowledge and the right tools.
- *Electrical:* Understanding basic electrical safety is crucial. While you should leave major electrical work to the professionals, you can safely perform minor tasks like replacing a light switch or installing a new light fixture.
- *General Repairs:* From patching drywall to resealing a window, general repair skills will come in handy on a regular basis. Make a habit of fixing problems when they're small to prevent them from becoming bigger issues later on.

Building, maintaining, and repairing your homestead is an ongoing task, but by developing these skills, you'll be better equipped to handle the challenges that come your way. Remember, a self-sufficient lifestyle doesn't mean doing everything yourself - it means having the knowledge and skills to handle tasks when you can, and knowing when to call in a professional.

SECTION 3: AMMO RELOADING AND GUNSMITHING

The ability to reload ammunition and maintain firearms is a highly practical skill for homesteaders who hunt for food, require pest control, or simply need to ensure their personal safety. It also offers a cost-effective alternative to purchasing new ammunition and opens opportunities for customization based on your needs.

Ammunition Reloading: Reloading ammunition involves reusing the spent shell casing and replacing the primer, powder, and bullet. This is typically done with a reloading press.

- **Safety First:** Always remember that you're dealing with materials that can explode if mishandled. Always follow safe practices, keep your reloading area clean, and pay attention to what you're doing. Wear eye protection and avoid smoking or having open flames nearby.
- **Understanding Components:** The four main components of a round of ammunition are the case, primer, powder, and bullet. Each component has numerous options depending on your firearm and what you'll be using the ammunition for. Familiarize yourself with the different types of each component and how they affect the performance of your ammunition.
- **The Reloading Process:** The basic process of reloading ammunition includes resizing and depriming the spent case, repriming the case, charging the case with powder, and seating and crimping the new bullet. You'll need a reloading press and the appropriate dies for your caliber.

Gunsmithing:

Gunsmithing is the art of maintaining, repairing, and modifying firearms. While detailed work should be left to professional gunsmiths, there are basic tasks every firearm owner should be able to perform.

- **Cleaning and Maintenance:** Regular cleaning and maintenance are crucial to keep your firearms operating reliably. You should know how to safely disassemble, clean, lubricate, and reassemble your firearms.
- **Simple Repairs:** Many common firearm problems can be solved with simple repairs. For example, you might need to replace a worn recoil spring or fix a loose sight.
- **Modifications:** Some firearm modifications can be performed at home with the right tools and knowledge. These might include fitting new grips or installing an accessory rail.

While these skills can seem daunting to learn, take it one step at a time. Invest in good tools, seek out reliable instructional resources, and always prioritize safety. Remember, "Knowledge is power. Information is liberating." - Kofi Annan. With the ability to reload ammunition and perform basic gunsmithing tasks, you'll not only increase your independence but also open up potential opportunities for trade in your community.

HOMESTEADING COMMERCE

Mastering various homesteading skills is not just crucial for the smooth operation and sustainability of your homestead, but these talents can also open up opportunities for business ventures and trade. Many skills like soap making, candle making, woodworking, brewing, baking, cheese making, and more have a potential market demand. By honing these skills, you can create artisanal, homemade products that are not only environmentally friendly but also high in quality and uniqueness, which can be sold locally at farmer's markets, online, or to neighbors and friends.

In addition to business potential, these skills can become invaluable in the aftermath of a major crisis or disaster. Should society face an event that disrupts conventional supply chains and systems of commerce, bartering skills and products would likely return as a primary form of exchange. The ability to produce something of value, whether it be food, clothing, tools, or other goods, will ensure your ability to acquire needed items that you cannot produce yourself. For instance, your home-brewed beer, handmade soap, or fresh produce might be traded for other essentials like medical supplies or firewood.

Beyond this, there is a deep satisfaction and sense of security that comes from mastering these skills. Knowing that you have the ability to provide for yourself and your family, regardless of external circumstances, is rewarding. This self-reliance is at the heart of homesteading and is a valuable asset in any situation.

Below is a list of 100 homesteading skills that could be invaluable should society come apart at the seams:

Skill	Skill	Skill	Skill
Cheese Making	Seed Saving	Foraging	Candle Making
Soap Making	Beekeeping	Wild Edible Identification	Basket Weaving
Canning	Quilting	Herb Identification	Tree Grafting

Skill	Skill	Skill	Skill
Fermenting	Knitting	Mushroom Identification	Raising Rabbits for Meat
Pickling	Crocheting	Animal Tracking	Natural Pest Control
Dehydrating Foods	Felting	Tanning Hides	Raised Bed Gardening
Bread Making	Blacksmithing	Fish Farming	Square Foot Gardening
Brewing Beer	Welding	Land Navigation	Goat Milking
Wine Making	Chainsaw Use & Maintenance	Weather Forecasting	Smokehouse Construction
Distilling Spirits	Firewood Processing	Rainwater Collection	Kombucha Brewing
Animal Husbandry	Composting	Well Digging	Making Tofu
Butchery	Natural Medicine Making	Windmill Construction	Scything
Fishing	Solar Panel Installation	Solar Oven Construction	Stone Wall Construction
Hunting	Knife Sharpening	Masonry	Making Vinegar
Trapping	Sausage Making	Carpentry	Animal Training
Food Foresting	Leather Working	Roof Repair	Winter Gardening
Aquaponics	Sourdough Starter Culturing	Gutter Installation	Tool Maintenance
Hydroponics	Bone Broth Making	Plumbing	Herbal Tea Brewing
Permaculture	Ham Radio Operation	Electrical Work	Vermiculture
Garden Planning	Greenhouse Operation	Composting Toilet Setup	Aquaculture
Seed Starting	Root Cellar Construction	Graywater System Setup	Ferret Training
Compost Making	Essential Oil Extraction	Off-Grid Laundry	Off-Grid Air Conditioning
Mulching	Rope Making	Biofuel Production	DIY Solar Shower
Tree Pruning	Macramé	Geothermal Setup	Outhouse Construction
Herbal Remedies	Soap Making	Chicken Tractor Building	Preserving Eggs

Homesteading Secrets of Our Ancestors | Page 58

CHAPTER 12: TAKING THE LEAP TO SELF-RELIANCE

Congratulations on reaching the end of this journey towards understanding the principles and practices of homesteading. Throughout this book, you've been introduced to a wealth of knowledge that will help you start your own homesteading journey and work towards becoming self-sufficient and off the grid.

You've learned about setting up your homestead, planning your garden, raising livestock, harnessing renewable energy, and acquiring a range of essential homesteading skills. All of this information might seem overwhelming, but remember: Rome wasn't built in a day, and neither will be your homestead.

As you venture into this exciting lifestyle, here are some actionable steps to help you move forward:

1. **Start with a Plan:** Use what you've learned to sketch out a blueprint for your homestead. Determine where you are now and where you want to be. Be realistic about your resources and limitations.
2. **Set Small, Achievable Goals:** Don't try to do everything at once. Start with a few key areas - perhaps setting up a small garden, or adding a few chickens to your homestead. As you achieve these small victories, you can gradually take on more.
3. **Learn by Doing:** There's no better way to learn than by getting your hands dirty. Whether it's planting your first seed or building your first chicken coop, the lessons you learn from practical experience will be invaluable.

4. **Network with Other Homesteaders:** Join local or online communities of like-minded individuals. Learn from their experiences and share your own. Remember, no one is an island, and we can all benefit from the wisdom and experience of others.
5. **Never Stop Learning:** The world of homesteading is vast and ever-changing. Always be open to new ideas, techniques, and technologies that can make your homesteading journey easier and more productive.

Remember, self-reliance doesn't mean you have to live in isolation or deprive yourself of modern comforts. It's about having control over your life and resources, understanding where your food comes from, and reducing your impact on the environment.

The path to self-reliance and off-the-grid living can be challenging, but it's also deeply rewarding. With every seed you sow, every animal you raise, and every renewable energy source you harness, you'll be living more in tune with nature and securing a sustainable future for yourself and your loved ones.

Remember, homesteading is not a race, but a journey, a lifestyle choice that's all about learning and growing. Every day brings a new challenge and a new opportunity. As you forge your path to self-reliance, keep your head high, your hands dirty, and your heart open to the endless possibilities that lie ahead.

So go forth, future homesteader, and carve out your piece of paradise. The future is in your hands.